Series / Number 07-071

ANALYZING COMPLEX SURVEY DATA

EUN SUL LEE
University of Texas
RONALD N. FORTHOFER
University of Texas
RONALD J. LORIMER
University of Texas

SAGE PUBLICATIONS
The Publishers of Professional Social Science
Newbury Park   London   New Delhi

For information address:

SAGE Publications, Inc.
2111 West Hillcrest Drive
Newbury Park, California 91320

SAGE Publications Ltd.
28 Banner Street
London EC1Y 8QE
England

SAGE Publications India Pvt. Ltd.
M-32 Market
Greater Kailash I
New Delhi 110 048 India

International Standard Book Number 0-8039-3014-3

Library of Congress Catalog Card No. 89-061127

FIRST PRINTING 1989

When citing a university paper, please use the proper form. Remember to cite the correct Sage University Paper series title and include the paper number. One of the following formats can be adapted (depending on the style manual used):

(1) IVERSEN, GUDMUND R. and NORPOTH, HELMUT (1976) "Analysis of Variance." Sage University Paper series on Quantitative Applications in the Social Sciences, 07-001. Beverly Hills: Sage Pubns.

OR

(2) Iversen, Gudmund R. and Norpoth, Helmut. 1976. Analysis of Variance. Sage University Paper series on Quantitative Applications in the Social Sciences, series no. 07-001. Beverly Hills: Sage Pubns.

CONTENTS

SERIES EDITOR'S INTRODUCTION*

Sample surveys are a major source of data for the modern social scientist. Researchers may analyze their own surveys or those that are publicly archived, for example, the National Opinion Research Center General Social Survey, the University of Michigan Institute for Social Research consumer and election surveys, the Research Triangle Institute surveys, the National Center for Health Statistics surveys, and the Census Bureau Current Population Survey. In the analysis of these surveys, the goal is usually to make inferences about population parameters, and the statistics routinely applied assume *simple random sampling* (SRS) with replacement was followed. Of course, this SRS assumption is almost never met, thus introducing another potential source of error into the analysis. Such surveys have a more complex design and better lend themselves to the particular techniques presented by Drs. Lee, Forthofer, and Lorimor.

To illustrate, suppose a national probability survey from the United States adult population was wanted. The researcher could not simply consult a list of American adults and execute, say, the *systematic selection procedure* (SSP), a useful variation on SRS. (Denmark may be a unique nation in having this type of listing for its citizenry.) Rather, what would be required is sampling that is *multistage* (e.g., ever smaller geographic units), *stratified* (e.g., grouped exhaustively by region), and *clustered* (e.g., in neighborhoods). Further, *weighting* (e.g., giving certain classes of respondents a different probability of selection) would undoubtedly be applied. (An introduction to survey sampling appears in the Kalton, 1983, series monograph.) Dr. Lee and his colleagues consider how to analyze complex surveys, focusing on the problems of weights and design effects. In data examples, they draw on the 1984 General Social Survey (National Opinion Research Center) and the second National Health and Nutrition Examination Survey (conducted by the National Center for Health Statistics in 1976-1980). They include a discussion of the choices involved in variance estimation and detail the different special computer programs available. By way of conclusion, they make a plea for more design-based, as opposed to model-based, statistical inference.

—*Michael S. Lewis-Beck*
Series Editor

*This volume was initially accepted by the former editors, Richard Niemi and John Sullivan.

ANALYZING COMPLEX SURVEY DATA

EUN SUL LEE
University of Texas

RONALD N. FORTHOFER
University of Texas

RONALD J. LORIMER
University of Texas

1. INTRODUCTION

Survey analysis is usually conducted as if all sample observations were independently selected with equal probabilities of selection. This analysis is correct if simple random sampling with replacement is used. However, in practice the sample selection is more complex than simple random sampling (SRS). Some sample observations may be weighted more heavily than others, and some are included in the sample by virtue of their membership in a certain group (e.g., household) rather than being selected independently. Can we simply ignore these departures from SRS in the analysis of survey data? Is it appropriate to use the standard techniques in statistics books and program packages for survey data analysis? Or, are there special methods and computer programs available for a more appropriate analysis of complex surveys? These questions are addressed in the following chapters.

The social survey today reflects a combination of statistical theory and knowledge about social phenomena, and its evolution has been shaped by experience gained from the conduct of many different surveys during the last 50 years. The social surveys were conducted to

AUTHORS' NOTE: *We are grateful to Robert E. Fay for providing an early version of PC CPLX program for log-linear models, to Tom W. Smith for answering questions about the sample design of General Social Survey, and to Richard G. Niemi for his support in the early stage of this project. Special thanks go to Barry I. Graubard, Lu Ann Aday, Michael S. Lewis-Beck, and the anonymous reviewers for their helpful comments and suggestions.*

7

meet the need for information to address social, political, and public health issues. Survey organizations were formed within and outside the government in response to this need for data. However, in the early attempts to provide the required information, the survey groups were mostly concerned with the practical issues in the field work, such as staff training and supervision, cost reduction, and sampling frame construction, and theoretical sampling issues received only secondary emphasis (Stephan, 1948). As these practical matters were resolved, modern sampling practice had developed far beyond simple random sampling. Complex sample designs had come to the fore and with them a number of analytic problems.

Since the early surveys generally needed only descriptive statistics, there was little interest in analytic problems. More recently, demands for analytic studies by social and policy scientists have increased, and available social survey data are analyzed to examine a variety of current issues by researchers who were not involved with the data collection process. This tradition is known as "secondary analysis" (Kendall and Lazarsfeld, 1950). However, often the researcher fails to pay due attention to the development of complex sample designs and assumes that these designs have little bearing on the analytic procedures to be used.

The increased use of statistical techniques in secondary analysis and the recent use of log-linear models and other multivariate techniques (Goodman, 1972a, 1972b, 1979; Swafford, 1980) have done little to bring design and analysis into closer alignment. These techniques are predicated on the use of simple random sampling with replacement (SRSWR). However, this assumption is rarely met in the social survey that employs stratification and clustering of observational units along with unequal probabilities of selection. As a result, the analysis of social surveys using the SRSWR assumption can lead to biased and misleading results. This problem is noted, for example, by Kiecolt and Nathan (1985) in their book on secondary analysis, but there is little guidance on how to incorporate the sample weights and other design features into the analysis.

Any survey that puts restrictions on the sampling beyond those of SRSWR is complex in design and requires special analytic considerations. This book reviews the analytic issues raised by the complex sample survey, provides an introduction to analytic strategies, and presents illustrations using some of the available software. Our discussion is centered around the use of the sample weights to correct for differential representations and the effect of sample designs on estimation of sampling error, with a brief treatment of poststratification adjustments. Many other important issues of nonsampling error are not addressed in this book.

In our presentation we are assuming some familiarity with sampling designs, such as simple random sampling without replacement (SRSWOR), stratified random sampling, and simple two-stage cluster sampling. A good presentation of these designs may be found in Kalton (1983).

2. SAMPLE DESIGN AND SURVEY DATA

Our consideration of survey data focuses on sample designs that satisfy two basic requirements. First, we are only concerned with probability sampling in which each element of a population has a known (nonzero) probability of being included in the sample. This is the basis for applying statistical theory in the derivation of the properties of the survey estimators for a given design. Second, if a sample is to be drawn from a population, it is necessary to be able to construct a sampling frame that lists suitable sampling units that encompass all elements of the population. If it is not feasible or is impractical to list all population elements, some clusters of the elements can be used as sampling units. For example, it is impractical to construct a list of all households in the United States, but we can select the sample in several stages. In the first stage, counties are randomly sampled; in the second stage, census tracts within the selected counties are sampled; in the third stage, street blocks are sampled within the selected tracts. Then the list of households is needed only for the selected blocks in the final stage of selection. This multistage design satisfies the requirement that all population elements have a known nonzero probability of being selected.

Types of Sampling

The simplest sample design is *simple random sampling,* which requires that each element have an equal probability of being included in the sample and that the list of all population elements is available. It can be carried out with or without replacement. Simple random sampling with replacement is of special interest because it simplifies statistical inference by eliminating any relation (covariance) between the selection of elements through the replacement process. In this scheme, however, an element can appear more than once in the sample. In practice, simple random sampling is carried out without replacement, since there is no need to collect the information more than once from an element. Additionally, SRSWOR gives a smaller sampling variance than SRSWR. However, these two sampling methods are practically the same in a large survey in which a small fraction of population elements are sampled. We will use the same "simple random sampling" (SRS) for the without replacement procedure throughout this book unless otherwise specified.

The SRS design is modified further to accommodate other theoretical and practical considerations. The common practical designs include systematic sampling, stratified random sampling, multistage cluster sampling, PPS (probability proportional to size) sampling, and other controlled selection procedures. These more practical designs deviate from SRS in two important ways. First, the inclusion probabilities for the elements (also the joint inclusion probabilities for sets of elements) may be unequal. Second, the sampling unit(s) can be different from the population element of interest. These departures complicate the usual methods of estimation and variance calculation and, if no adjustments are made, can lead to a bias in estimation and statistical tests. We will consider these departures in detail, using several specific sample designs, and examine their implications for survey analysis.

Systematic sampling is commonly used as an alternative to SRS because of its simplicity. It selects every k-th element after a random start. Its procedural tasks are simple and the process can easily be checked, whereas it is difficult to verify SRS by examining the results. It is often used in the final stage of multistage sampling when the field worker is instructed to select a predetermined proportion of units from the listing of dwellings in a street block. The systematic sampling procedure assigns each element in a population the same probability of being selected. This assures that the sample mean will be an unbiased estimate of the population mean when the number of elements in the population (N) is equal to k times the number of elements in the sample (n). However, it can give an unrealistic estimate when the elements in the frame are listed in a cyclical manner with respect to a survey variable and the selection interval coincides with the listing cycle. For example, if one selects every 40th patient coming to a clinic and the average daily patient load is about 40, then the resulting sample would contain only those who came to the clinic at a certain time of the day. Such a sample may not be representative of the clinic patients.

Moreover, even when the listing is randomly ordered, unlike SRS, different sets of elements may have unequal inclusion probabilities. For example, the probability of including both the i-th and $(i+k)$-th element is $1/k$ in a systematic sample, whereas the probability of including both the i-th and $(i+k+1)$-th is zero. This complicates the variance calculation. Another way of viewing systematic sampling is that it is equivalent to selecting one cluster from k systematically formed clusters of n elements each. The sampling variance (between clusters) cannot be estimated from the one cluster selected. Thus, variance estimation from a systematic sample requires special strategies.

A modification to overcome these problems with systematic sampling is the so-called repeated systematic sampling (Levy and Lemeshow, 1980: 80-84). Instead of taking a systematic sample in one pass through the list, several smaller systematic samples are selected going down the list several times with a new starting point in each pass. This procedure not only guards against possible periodicity in the frame but also allows variance estimation directly from the data. The variance of an estimate from all subsamples can be estimated from the variability of the separate estimates from each subsample. This idea of replicated sampling offers a strategy for estimating variance for complex surveys, which will be discussed further in Chapter 4.

Stratified sampling classifies the population elements into strata and samples separately from each stratum. It is used for several reasons: (1) the sampling variance can be reduced if the strata are internally homogeneous; (2) separate estimates with predetermined precision can be obtained for strata; (3) administration of the field work can be organized using the strata; and (4) different sampling needs can be accommodated in separate strata. Allocation of the sample across the strata is proportionate when the sampling fraction is uniform across the strata or disproportionate when, for instance, a higher sampling fraction is applied to a smaller stratum to select a sufficient number of subjects for comparative studies. In general, the estimation process for a stratified sample is more complicated than in SRS. It is generally described as a two-step process. The first step is the calculation of the statistics, for example, the mean and its variance separately within each stratum. These estimates are then combined based on weights reflecting the proportion of the population in each stratum. As will be discussed later, it can also be described as a one-step process using weighted statistics. The estimation simplifies in the case of proportionate stratified sampling, but the strata must be taken into account in the variance estimation.

The formulation of the strata requires that information on the stratification variables be available for the sampling frame. When stratification is desired, but such information is not available, poststratification can be used. It is used to make the sample more representative of the population by adjusting the demographic composition of the sample to the census population. Typically, such demographic variables as age, sex, race, and education are used in poststratification. This adjustment requires the use of weights and complicates the estimation process, especially the variance estimation.

Cluster sampling is often a more practical approach to surveys because it samples by groups (clusters) of elements rather than by individual elements. It is especially true in constructing sampling frames and saving survey costs. Often a hierarchy of geographical clusters is used, as described earlier. In multistage cluster sampling, the sampling units are groups of elements except for the last stage of sampling. When the number of elements in the clusters are equal, the estimation process is equivalent to SRS. However, simple random sampling of unequal-sized clusters leads to the elements in the smaller clusters being more likely to be in the sample than those in the larger clusters. Additionally, the clusters are often stratified to accomplish certain survey objectives and field procedures, for instance, the oversampling of predominantly black clusters. The use of disproportionate stratification and unequal-sized clusters complicates the estimation process.

One method to draw a self-weighting sample of elements in one-stage cluster sampling of unequal size clusters is to sample clusters with probability proportional to the size of clusters (PPS sampling). However, this requires that the true size of clusters be known. Since the true sizes are usually unknown at the time of the survey, the selection probability is instead made proportional to the estimated size (PPES sampling). For example, the number of beds can be used as a measure of size in a survey of hospital discharges with hospitals as the clusters. One important consequence of PPES sampling is that the expected sample size will vary from one PSU (primary sampling unit) to another. In other words, the sample size is not fixed but varies from sample to sample. Therefore, the sample size, the denominator in the calculation of a sample mean, is a random variable, and, hence, the sample mean becomes a ratio of two random variables. This type of variable, a ratio variable, requires special strategies for variance estimation.

The Nature of Survey Data

If we are to infer from sample to population, the sample selection process is an integral part of the inference process, and the survey data must contain information on important dimensions of the selection process. Considering the departures from SRS in most social surveys, we need to view the survey data not only as records of measurements, but also as having different representation and structural arrangements.

Sample weights are used to reflect the differing probabilities of selection of the sample elements. The development of sample weights requires keeping track of selection probabilities separately in each stratum and at each stage of sampling. In addition, it can involve correcting for differential response rates within classes of the sample and adjusting the sample distribution by demographic variables to known population distributions. Moreover, different sample weights are needed for different units of analysis. For instance, in a community survey it may be necessary to develop person weights and household weights.

We may feel secure in the exclusion of the weights when one of the following self-weighting designs is used. True PPS sampling in a one-stage cluster sampling will produce a self-weighting sample of elements, as in the SRS design. The self-weighting can also be accomplished in a two-stage design when true PPS sampling is used in the first stage and a fixed number of units are selected in each selected PSU. The same result will follow if simple random sampling is used in the first stage and a fixed proportion of the units are selected in the second stage (see Kalton, 1983, Chapters 5 and 6). But, in practice, the self-weighting feature is destroyed by nonresponse and possible errors in the sampling frame(s). This unintended self-selection process can introduce bias, but it is seldom possible to assess the bias from an examination of the sample data. Two methods employed in an attempt to reduce the bias are poststratification and nonresponse adjustments. Poststratification involves assigning the weights to bring the sample proportion in demographic subgroups into agreement with the population proportion in the subgroups. Nonresponse adjustment inflates the weights for those who participate in the survey to account for the nonrespondents with similar characteristics. Because of the nonresponse and poststratification adjustments by weighting, the use of weights is almost unavoidable even when a self-weighting design is used.

The sample design affects the estimation of standard errors and, hence, must also be incorporated into the analysis. A close examination of the familiar formulas for standard errors in statistics textbooks and incorporated into most computer program packages shows that they are based on the SRSWR design. These formulas are relatively simple because the covariance between elements is zero, due to the assumed independent selection of elements. It is not immediately evident how the formulas should be modified to adjust for other sampling designs.

To better understand the need for adjustment to the variance formulas, we first examine the variance formula for a sample mean from the SRSWOR design. The familiar variance formula for a sample mean, $\bar{y}$ (selecting a sample of n elements from a population of N elements by SRSWR where the population mean is $\bar{Y}$) in elementary statistics textbooks is

$$\sigma^2/n \text{ where } \sigma^2 = \sum (Y_i - \bar{Y})^2/n \text{ or}$$
$$(N-1)S^2/nN \text{ where } S^2 = \sum (Y_i - \bar{Y})^2/(N-1)$$

This formula needs to be modified for the SRSWOR design, since the selection of an element is no longer independent of the selection of another element. Because duplicate selections are not allowed, there is a covariance between sample elements. The covariance turns out to be negative $(-(n-1)\sigma^2/2n(N-1)$ or $-(n-1)S^2/2nN)$. Then, the variance of the sample mean from SRSWOR can be obtained by combining the variance from SRSWR and twice the negative covariance, which yields $(N-n)\sigma^2/n(N-1)$ or $(N-n)S^2/nN$. Because of the negative covariance, the variance from SRSWOR is smaller than that from SRSWR by the factor of $(N-n)/(N-1)$ in terms of σ^2 or in terms of S^2, $(N-n)/N$. The quantity $(N-n)/N$ is also written $(1-f)$ where $f = n/N$. Either of $(N-n)/(N-1)$ or $(1-f)$ is called the finite population correction (fpc). In a large population the covariance will be very small. When the sampling fraction (n/N) is small, SRSWR and SRSWOR designs will produce practically the same variance and can be considered equivalent for all practical purposes.

Stratified sampling is often presented as a more efficient design because, if used appropriately, it gives a smaller variance than that given by a comparable SRS. Since the covariances between strata are zero, the variance of the sample estimate is derived from the within-strata variances, which are combined based on the stratum sample sizes and the stratum weights. The value of stratified sample variance depends on the distribution of the strata sample sizes. An optimal (or Neyman) allocation produces a sampling variance less than or equal to that based on SRS except in extremely rare situations. For other disproportionate allocations, the sampling variance may turn out to be larger than that based on SRS when the finite population correction factor within strata cannot be ignored. Therefore, it cannot be assumed that stratification will always reduce sampling variance compared to SRS.

The cluster sampling design usually leads to a larger sampling variance compared to SRS. This is because the elements within naturally formed clusters are often similar, which then yields a positive covariance between elements within the cluster. The homogeneity within clusters is measured by the intraclass correlation coefficient (ICC)—the correlation between all possible pairs of elements within clusters. If clusters were randomly formed (i.e., if each cluster were a random sample of elements), the ICC would be zero. In many natural clusters the ICC is positive and, hence, the sampling variance will be larger than that for the SRS design.

It is difficult to generalize regarding the relative size of the sampling variance in a complex design because the combined effects of stratification and clustering, as well as that of the sample weights, must be assessed. Therefore, all observations in survey data must be viewed as products of a specific sample design that contains sample weights and structural arrangements. In addition to the sample weights, strata and cluster identification (at least PSU) should be included in sample survey data. Reasons for these requirements will become clearer later.

One complication in the variance calculation for a complex survey stems from the use of weights. Because the sum of weights in the denominator of any weighted estimator is not fixed but varies from sample to sample, the estimator becomes a ratio of two random variables. In general, a ratio estimator is biased, but the bias is negligible if the variation in the weights is relatively small or the sample size is large (Cochran, 1977, Chapter 6). Thus, the problem of bias in the ratio estimator is not an issue in large social surveys. Because of this bias, however, it is appropriate to use the mean square error—the sum of the variance and the square of the bias—rather than the variance. However, since the bias is often negligible, we will use the term "variance" even if we are referring to mean square error in this book.

3. SURVEY DATA ANALYSIS

This chapter introduces the concept of weights and discusses the effect of sample selection designs on variance estimation. An appreciation of both the weighting procedures and the design effect concept (defined below) is required for the analysis of complex survey data.

Adjusting for Differential Representation: The Weight

Two types of sample element weights are commonly encountered in the analysis of survey data: (1) the expansion weight, which is the reciprocal of the selection probability, and (2) the relative weight, which is obtained by adjusting the expansion weight to reflect sample size. This section reviews these two types of weights in detail for several sample designs.

Consider the following SRS situation: A list of all 4,000 elements in a population is numbered from 1 to N. A table of random numbers is used to draw a fixed number of elements (for example, $n = 200$) from the population without replacement. Then the selection probability or sampling fraction is $f = n/N = 0.05$. The expansion weight is the reciprocal of the selection probability, $w_i = 1/f = N/n = 20$ ($i = 1, \ldots, n$), and these weights for the n elements selected sum to N. An estimator of the population total of variable Y based on the sample elements is

$$\hat{Y} = \sum w_i y_i = (N/n) \sum y_i = N \bar{y}. \qquad [3.1]$$

Equation 3.1 shows the use of the expansion weight in the weighted sum of sample observations. Since the weight is the same for each element in SRS, the estimator can be simplified to N times the sample mean (the last quantity in equation 3.1). Similarly, the estimator of the population mean is defined to be $\hat{Y} = \Sigma w_i y_i / \Sigma w_i$, a weighted average. In SRS this simplifies to $(N/n)\Sigma y_i / N = \bar{y}$, showing that the sample mean is an estimator for the population mean. However, even if the weights are not the same (in unequal probability designs), the estimators are still a weighted sum for the population total and a weighted average for the population mean.

While the expansion weight appears reasonable for the estimator of the population, it may play havoc with the average and other statistical measures. Using the sum of expansion weights ($\Sigma w_i = N$) in the denominator in place of the sample size causes many computer programs to err in the calculation of variance used in test statistics and confidence intervals. To deal with this, the expansion weight is often adjusted to produce a relative weight, rw_i, which is defined to be the expansion weight divided by the mean of the expansion weights, that is, $w_i/\bar{w}$ where $\bar{w} = \Sigma w_i/n$. For the SRS design, rw_i is one for each sample element, and the sum of the relative weights over all the sample elements is the sample size, n. The relative weighted estimator for the population total is

$$\hat{Y} = \bar{w} \Sigma rw_i y_i = (N/n) \Sigma y_i = N\bar{y}. \qquad [3.2]$$

Note in equation 3.2 that the relative weighted sum is multiplied by the average expansion weight, which yields the same simplified estimator for the case of SRS as in equation 3.1. Hence, the expansion weight is simpler to use than the relative weight in estimating the population total and, thus, is used more often in descriptive surveys. However, in the cross-tabulation of variables, the cell frequencies add up to N when the expansion weights are used and to n when the relative weights are used. Statistical inference would be misleading if based on a total assuming N observations when only n observations were collected. Therefore, the relative weight is more appropriately used in analytic studies based on frequency data.

Let us consider expansion weights in a stratified random sampling design. Often the population of N elements is grouped into L strata based on some variable with $N_1, N_2, \ldots N_L$ elements respectively from which n_h ($h = 1, 2, \ldots, L$) elements are independently selected from the h-th stratum. A stratified design retains a self-weighting quality when the sampling fraction in each stratum is the same, i.e., $n_h/N_h = f_h = n/N = f$. If a total of 200 elements are proportionately selected from two strata of $N_1 = 600$ and $N_2 = 3400$ elements, then $f = 200/4000 = 0.05$. A proportionate selection (a 5 percent sample from each stratum) yields $n_1 = 30$ and $n_2 = 170$ since $f_1 = 30/600 = 0.05$ and $f_2 = 170/3400 = 0.05$. The weighting scheme is then exactly the same as described above for the SRS design.

The situation is slightly different with a disproportionate stratified sample design. For example, if the total sample of 200 were split equally between the two strata, $f_1 (= 100/600)$ and $f_2 (= 100/3400)$ have different values and the expansion weights are unequal for the elements in the two strata, with $w_{1i} = 6$ and $w_{2i} = 34$. The expansion weights sum to 600 in the first stratum and to 3400 in the second, with their total being 4000, the population size. The mean expansion weight, $\overline{w} = (100 \times 6 + 100 \times 34)/200 = 20$, and, hence, the relative weights sum to 30 in the first stratum and to 170 in the second, i.e., to the sample sizes. Note that the use of either type of weight is equivalent to weighting stratum means $(\overline{y}_h)$ using the population distribution across the strata (i.e., $\Sigma (N_h/N)\overline{y}_h$, the standard procedure). Both the expansion and relative weights in stratum 1 sum to 15 percent of their respective total sums, and the first stratum also contains 15 percent of the population elements.

Although we have used SRS and stratified sample designs to introduce the sample weights, the same concept extends easily to more complex designs. In summary, the sample weight is the inverse of the selection probability, although it often is further modified by poststratification and nonresponse adjustments. The assignment of the sample weight to each sample element facilitates a general estimation procedure for all sample designs. As a general rule, all estimates take the form of weighted statistics in survey analysis. The weight is usually calculated as the expansion weight aligned to the population size, but it can easily be converted to the relative weight aligned to the sample size.

Developing the Weight: An Example

To demonstrate the development of sample weights, we shall work with the 1984 General Social Survey (GSS). This is a complex sample survey conducted by the National Opinion Research Center (NORC) to obtain general social information from the civilian noninstitutionalized adult population (18 years of age and older) of the United States. A multistage selection design was used to produce a self-weighting sample at the household level. One adult was then randomly selected from each sampled household (Davis and Smith,

1985). There were 1,473 observations available for analysis in the data file. For the purpose of illustration, the expansion weight for these data at the household level could be calculated by dividing the number of households in the United States by 1,473. The expansion weight within the sampled household is the number of adults in the household. The product of these two weights gives the expansion weight for sample individuals.

For an analysis of the GSS data, we need to focus only on the weight within the household, since each household has the same probability of selection. The relative weight for the individual can be derived by dividing the number of adults in the household by the average number of adults (2852/1473 = 1.94) per household. This weight reflects the probability of selection of an individual in the sample while preserving the sample size.

We further modified this weight by a poststratification adjustment in an attempt to make the sample composition the same as the population composition. This would improve the precision of estimates and could possibly reduce nonresponse and sample selection bias to the extent that it is related to the demographic composition.[1] As shown in Table 3.1, the adjustment factor is derived to cause the distribution of individuals in the sample to match the 1984 U.S. population by age, race, and sex. Column 1 is the 1984 population distribution by race, sex, and age, based on the Census Bureau's estimates. Column 2 shows the weighted number of adults in the sampled households by the demographic subgroups, and the proportional distribution is in Column 3. The adjustment factor is the ratio of Column 1 to Column 3. The adjusted weight is found by multiplying the adjustment factor by the relative weight, and the distribution of adjusted weights is then the same as the population distribution. The adjustment factors indicate that without the adjustment the GSS sample underrepresents males 25-34 years of age and overrepresents nonwhite males 45-54 years of age and nonwhite females 25-34 years of age.

The adjusted relative weights are then used in the analysis of the data, for example, to estimate the proportion of adults responding positively to the question: "Are there any situations that you can imagine in which you would approve of a man punching an adult male stranger?" The weighting option is available in most statistical program packages (e.g., WEIGHT in SAS and WEIGHT BY in SPSSX). As shown in the upper panel of Table 3.2, the weighted overall proportion is 60.0 percent, slightly larger than the unweighted esti-

TABLE 3.1

Derivation of Poststratification Adjustment Factor:
General Social Survey, 1984

Demographic Subgroups	Population Distribution* (1)	Weighted No. of Adults in Sample (2)	Sample Distribution (3)	Adjustment Factor (1) / (3)
White, male				
18 – 24 yrs	.0719660	211	.9739832	.9727346
25 – 34	.1028236	193	.0676718	1.5194460
35 – 44	.0708987	277	.0795933	.8907624
45 – 54	.0557924	135	.0473352	1.1786660
55 – 64	.0544026	144	.0504909	1.0774730
65 & over	.0574872	138	.0483871	1.1880687
White, female				
18 – 24	.0705058	198	.0694250	1.1555680
25 – 34	.1007594	324	.1136045	.8869317
35 – 44	.0777364	267	.0936185	.8303528
45 – 54	.0582026	196	.0682737	.8469074
55 – 64	.0610057	186	.0652174	.9354210
65 & over	.0823047	216	.0757363	1.0867272
Nonwhite, male				
18 – 24	.0138044	34	.0119215	1.1579480
25 – 34	.0172057	30	.0105189	1.6356880
35 – 44	.0109779	30	.0105189	1.0436290
45 – 54	.0077643	37	.0129734	.5984774
55 – 64	.0064683	12	.0042076	1.5372900
65 & over	.0062688	18	.0063113	.9932661
Nonwhite, female				
18 – 24	.0145081	42	.0145081	.9851716
25 – 34	.0196276	86	.0301543	.6509067
35 – 44	.0130655	38	.0133240	.9806026
45 – 54	.0094590	33	.0115708	.8174809
55 – 64	.0079636	30	.0105189	.7570769
65 & over	.0090016	27	.0094670	.9508398
Total	1.0000000	2852	1.0000000	

*Based on noninstitutional population; Source: U.S. Bureau of the Census, "Estimates of the population of the United States, by age, sex, and race, 1980 to 1985," Current Population Reports, Series P-25 (No. 985), April, 1986; derived from the estimated total population of 1984 (Table 1) adjusted by applying the ratio of noninstitutional to total population (Table A1).

mate of 59.4 percent. The difference between the weighted and unweighted estimates is also very small for the subgroup estimates shown. This may be due primarily to the self-weighting feature reflected in the fact that most households have two adults and, to a lesser extent, to the fact that the "approval of hitting" is not corre-

TABLE 3.2

Comparison of Weighted and Unweighted Estimates in Two Surveys

Survey	Variables	Weighted Estimate	Unweighted Estimate
I. General Social Survey (percent approving "hitting")			
Overall		60.0	59.4
by sex			
Male		63.5	63.2
Female		56.8	56.8
by education			
Some college		68.7	68.6
High school		63.3	63.2
Others		46.8	45.2
II. Epidemiologic Catchment Area Survey* (prevalence of mental disorders)			
Any disorders		14.8	18.5
Anxiety disorders		6.5	8.8

*Source: Lee et al. (1986b), Table 1.

lated with the number of adults in a household. The situation is different in the National Institute of Mental Health sponsored Epidemiologic Catchment Area Survey. In this survey, the weighted estimates of the prevalence of any disorders or of anxiety disorders are 20 or 26 percent lower than the unweighted estimates (see the lower panel of Table 3.2).

Assessing Loss or Gain of Precision: The Design Effect

As shown in the previous chapter, the variance of an SRSWOR sample mean is the variance of an SRSWR sample mean times the finite population correction factor $(1-f)$. The ratio of sampling variance of SRSWOR to the sampling variance of SRSWR is then $(1-f)$, which reflects the effect of using SRSWOR compared to SRSWR. This ratio comparing the variance of some statistic from any particular design to that of SRSWR is called the design effect for that statistic. It is used to assess the loss or gain in precision of sample estimates from the design used compared to a SRSWR design. A ratio less than one indicates that fewer observations are needed to achieve the same precision as SRSWR, whereas a ratio greater than one indicates that more observations are needed to yield the same precision.

In the case of SRSWOR, the design effect is less than one, but it is close to one when the sampling fraction is very small.

Because SRSWOR is customarily used in place of SRSWR, researchers have tended to base the design effect calculation on SRSWOR instead of SRSWR. In addition, in complex surveys the design effect is usually calculated based on the variance of the weighted statistic under the SRSWOR design. We shall do that throughout the rest of the book.

Relating this notion of the design effect to the sample size, the effective sample size can be defined to be the actual sample size divided by the design effect. If a design effect is greater than one for a sample design, then, in effect, the sample size would be reduced for a statistical analysis.

Let us examine the design effect in more complex sample designs. The properties and estimation of sampling error for stratified random sampling are well known and so are the conditions under which stratification will produce a smaller variance than SRS. However, stratification often is used in conjunction with other design features, such as cluster sampling in several stages within the strata. As discussed earlier, clustering tends to increase sampling error. The effect of stratification can be diluted by the effect of clustering in many practical designs. Unfortunately, the assessment of design effect cannot be determined theoretically from properties of stratification and clustering separately, but must be approximated numerically to account for their combined effects.

The following example demonstrates the determination of the design effect in a relatively simple situation. Consider the case of single-stage cluster sampling where all clusters are of the same size. Suppose that there are N English classes (clusters) in a high school with M students in each class. From the N classes, n classes are selected by SRS, and all the students in the chosen clusters are asked to report the number of books they have read since the beginning of the year. The number of students is NM in the population and nM in the sample. The sampling fraction is $f = nM/NM = n/N$. Since the class sizes are equal, the average number of books read per student (the population mean) is the mean of the N class means, $\bar{Y}_i$. The n sample classes can be viewed as a random sample of n means from a population of N means. Therefore, the sample mean $\bar{\bar{y}}$ is unbiased for the population mean $\bar{\bar{Y}}$ and its variance is given by

$$V(\bar{\bar{y}}) = \{(1-f)\, S_b^{\,2}/n \qquad\qquad [3.3]$$

where $S_b^{\,2} = \Sigma\,(\bar{Y}_i - \bar{\bar{Y}}\,)^2/(N-1)$, the variance of the cluster means. Alternately, equation 3.3 can be expressed in terms of the intraclass correlation coefficient (ICC), ρ, as follows (Cochran, 1977, Chapter 9):

$$V(\bar{\bar{y}}) = (1-f)\, S^2\,[\,1 + (M-1)\,\rho]/nM. \qquad\qquad [3.4]$$

This can be compared to the variance of the mean from an SRSWOR sample of size nM, $(1-f)S^2/nM$, and the design effect of the cluster sample is then $1 + (M-1)\rho$.

When $\rho = 0$ the design effect will be one; when $\rho > 0$ the design effect will be greater than one. If the clusters were formed at random, then $\rho = 0$; when all the elements within each cluster have the same value, $\rho = 1$. Most clusters used in community surveys consist of houses in the same area, and these yield small positive ICCs for many survey variables. The ICC is usually somewhat larger for socioeconomic variables than for the demographic variables, such as age and sex.

The assessment of the design effect for a more complex sample design is not a routine task that can be performed using the formulas in statistics textbooks; rather, it requires special techniques that utilize unfamiliar strategies. The next chapter reviews several strategies of estimating the sampling variance for statistics from complex surveys and examines the design effect from several surveys.

4. STRATEGIES FOR VARIANCE ESTIMATION

The variance estimation of a survey statistic is complicated not only by the nature of the sampling design, as seen in the previous chapters, but also by the form of the statistic. Even with an SRS design, the variance estimation of some statistics requires nonstandard estimating techniques. For example, the variance of the median is conspicuously absent in the standard texts; the standard variance formulas are not available for such complicated statistics as the odds ratio and other nonlinear statistics; and the sampling error of a ratio estimator[2] is complicated because both the numerator and denominator are random variables. Ratio estimators are widely used by government agencies to obtain more accurate estimates. Certain variance estimating techniques not found in the standard textbooks are sufficiently flexible to accommodate both the complexities of the sampling design and the various forms of statistics. These general techniques for variance estimation to be reviewed in this chapter are Replicated Sampling, Balanced Repeated Replication, Jackknife Repeated Replication, and the Taylor Series Method.

Replicated Sampling: A General Approach

The essence of this strategy is to facilitate the variance calculation by selecting a set of replicated subsamples instead of a single sample. It requires each subsample to be drawn independently and to use an identical sample selection design. Then an estimate is made in each subsample by the identical process, and the sampling variance of the overall estimate (based on all subsamples) can be estimated from the variability of these independent subsample estimates. This is the same idea as the repeated systematic sampling mentioned in Chapter 2.

The sampling variance of the mean $(\bar{u})$ of t replicate estimates $u_1, u_2, \ldots, u_t$ of the parameter U can be estimated by this simple variance estimator (see Kalton, 1983: 51):

$$v(\bar{u}) = \sum (u_i - \bar{u})^2 / t(t-1).$$ [4.1]

This estimator can be applied to any sample statistic obtained from independent replicates of any sample design.

In applying this variance estimator, ten replicates are recommended by Deming (1960) and a minimum of four by others (Sudman, 1976) for descriptive statistics. An approximate estimate of standard error can be calculated by dividing the range in the replicate estimates by the number of replicates when the number of replicates is between 3 and 13 (Kish, 1965: 620). However, since this variance estimator with t replicates is then based on $(t-1)$ degrees of freedom for statistical inference, a larger number of replicates may be needed for analytic studies, perhaps 20 to 30 (Kalton, 1983: 52).

In practical applications, the fundamental principles of selecting independent replicates are somewhat relaxed. For one thing, replicates are selected using sampling without replacement instead of with replacement. For unequal probability designs, the calculation of basic weights and the adjustment for nonresponse and poststratification are usually performed only once for the full sample, rather than separately within each replicate. In cluster sampling, the replicates are often formed by systematically assigning the clusters to the t replicates in the same order that the clusters were first selected to take advantage of stratification effects. In applying equation 4.1, the sample mean from the full sample is generally used for the mean of the replicate means. These deviations from fundamental principles can affect the variance estimation, but the bias is thought to be insignificant in large-scale surveys (Wolter, 1985: 83-85).

The community mental health survey conducted in New Haven, Connecticut, in 1984 as part of the Epidemiologic Catchment Area program of the National Institute of Mental Health (Lee et al., 1986a) provides an example of replicated sampling. The sampling frame for this survey was a geographically ordered list of residential electric hookups. A systematic sample was drawn by taking two housing units as a cluster with an interval of 61 houses, using a starting point chosen at random. A string of clusters in the sample was then sequentially allocated to 12 subsamples. These subsamples were created to facilitate the scheduling and interim analysis of data during a long period of screening and interviewing. Ten of the subsamples were used for the community survey with the remaining two reserved for another study. The ten replicates are used to illustrate the variance estimation procedure.

These subsamples did not strictly adhere to a fundamental principle of independent replicated sampling since the starting points were systematically selected, except for the first random starting point. However, the systematic allocation of clusters to subsamples in this case introduced an approximate stratification leading to a more stable variance estimation and, therefore, may be preferable to a random selection of a starting point for this relatively small number of replicates. Therefore, we considered these subsamples as replicates and applied the variance estimator with replicated sampling, equation 4.1.

Since one adult was randomly selected from each sampled household using the Kish selection table (Kish, 1949), the number of adults in each household became the sample case weight for each observation. This weight was then adjusted for nonresponse and poststratification. Sample weights were developed for the full sample, not separately within each subsample, and these were the weights used in the analysis.

Table 4.1 shows three types of statistics calculated for the full sample as well as for each of the replicates. The estimated standard error of the prevalence rate (p) can be calculated from the replicate esti-

TABLE 4.1
Estimation of Standard Errors from Replicates (n = 3,058)

			Selected Statistics			
Replicate	Prevalence Rate*	Odds Ratio**	Intercept	Regression Gender	Coefficients+ Color	Age
Full sample	17.17	0.990	0.2237	–0.0081	0.0185	–0.0020
1	12.81	0.826	0.2114	0.0228	0.0155	–0.0020
2	17.37	0.844	0.2581	0.0220	0.0113	–0.0027
3	17.87	1.057	0.2426	–0.0005	0.0393	–0.0015
4	17.64	0.638	0.1894	0.0600	0.2842	–0.0029
5	16.65	0.728	0.1499	0.0448	–0.0242	–0.0012
6	18.17	1.027	0.2078	–0.0024	–0.0030	–0.0005
7	14.69	1.598	0.3528	–0.0487	–0.0860	–0.0028
8	17.93	1.300	0.3736	–0.0333	–0.0629	–0.0032
9	17.86	0.923	0.2328	0.0038	0.0751	–0.0015
10	18.91	1.111	0.3008	–0.0007	0.0660	–0.0043
Range	6.10	0.960	0.2237	0.1087	0.3702	0.0038

Standard error based on:

Replicates	0.59	0.090	0.0234	0.0104	0.0324	0.0004
SRS	0.68	0.097	0.0228	0.0141	0.0263	0.0004

 * Percent with any mental disorders during the last 6 months.
** Sex difference in the 6-month prevalence rate.
 + The dependent variable (coded as 1 = condition present and
   0 = condition absent) is regressed on sex (1 = male; 0 = female),
   color (1 = black; 0 = nonblack), and age (continuous variable).
   This analysis is used for demonstration only.

Source: Reprinted by permission of the publisher from Lee et al. (1986a).

mates (p_i) using equation 4.1: $v(p) = \Sigma (p_i - 17.17)^2 / 10 (10 - 1) =$ 0.59. The overall prevalence rate of 17.17 percent is slightly different from the mean of the ten replicate estimates due to the differences in response rates. Note that one-tenth of the range in the replicate estimates (0.61) approximates the standard error obtained by equation 4.1. Similarly, standard errors can be estimated for the odds ratio and regression coefficients. The estimated standard errors have approximately the same values as those calculated by assuming simple random sampling (using appropriate formulas from textbooks). This indicates that design effects are fairly small for these statistics from this survey.

Although the replicated sampling design provides a variance estimator that is simple, it requires a sufficient number of replicates to obtain acceptable precision for statistical inference. But if there are a large number of replicates and each replicate is relatively small, it severely limits using stratification in each replicate. For these reasons, a replicated design is seldom used in large-scale, analytic surveys; instead, in practice, replicated sampling has evolved into pseudo-replication techniques that overcome some of these difficulties. The next two techniques are based on this idea of pseudo-replication.

Balanced Repeated Replication

The balanced repeated replication (BRR) method is based on the application of the replicated sampling idea to a paired selection design in which two units are sampled from each stratum. The paired selection design represents the maximum use of stratification and yet allows the calculation of variance. In this case, the variance between two units is one-half of the squared difference between them. To apply the replicated sampling idea, we first divide the sample into random groups to form replicates (pseudo-replication). If it is a stratified design, it requires all the strata to be represented in each pseudo-replicate. In a stratified, paired selection design, we can form only two pseudo-replicates: one containing one of the two units from each stratum and the other containing the remaining unit from each stratum (complement replicate). Each pseudo-replicate then includes approximately one-half of the total sample. Applying equation 4.1 with $t = 2$, we can estimate the sampling variance of the mean of the two replicate estimates u', u'' by

$$v(\bar{u}) = [(u' - \bar{u})^2 + (u'' - \bar{u})^2]/2. \qquad [4.2]$$

As in the previous section, the mean of replicate estimates is often replaced by an overall estimate obtained from the full sample.

However, this variance estimator is too unstable to have any practical value since it is based on only two pseudo-replicates. The BRR method solves this by repeating the process of forming half samples from the full original sample. Different units from different strata can be combined in each pseudo-replicate. The pseudo-replicated half samples then contain some common units, and this introduces dependence between replicates which complicates the variance estimation.

One solution, which leads to unbiased estimates of variance for linear statistics, is to balance the formation of pseudo-replicates by using an orthogonal matrix (Plackett and Burman, 1946). The full balancing requires that the size of the matrix be a multiple of four and the number of replicates be greater than or equal to the number of strata.

Then the sampling variance of a sample statistic can be estimated by taking the average of variance estimates by equation 4.2 over t pseudo-replicates:

$$\mathrm{v}\,(\,\bar{u}\,) = \sum\,[\,(\,u'_i - \bar{u}\,)^2 + (\,u''_i - \bar{u}\,)^2\,]/2t = \sum\,(\,u'_i - u''_i\,)^2/4t. \quad [4.3]$$

It is possible to reduce computation by dropping the complement half-sample replicates:

$$\mathrm{v}^*\,(\,\bar{u}\,) = \sum\,(\,u'_i - \bar{u}\,)^2/t, \quad\quad\quad [4.4]$$

this is the variance estimator originally proposed by McCarthy (1966). As was mentioned above, this balancing was shown by McCarthy to yield unbiased estimates of variance for linear estimators. For nonlinear estimators there is a bias in the estimates of variance, but numerical studies suggest that it is small. For a large number of strata, the computational cost can be further reduced by using a set of partially balanced replicates (Lee, 1972; Wolter, 1985: 125-130).

As in replicated sampling, BRR assumes that the PSUs are sampled with replacement within strata, although in practice sampling without replacement is generally used. Theoretically, this leads to an overestimation of variance when applied to a sample selected without replacement, but the overestimation is negligible in practice since the chance of selecting the same unit more than once under sampling without replacement is low when the sampling fraction is small. The sampling fraction in a paired selection design (assumed in the BRR method) is usually small because only two PSUs are selected from each stratum.

When used with a multistage selection design, BRR is usually applied only to the primary sampling units (PSUs) and disregards the subsampling within the PSUs. Such a practice is predicated on the fact that the sampling variance can be approximated adequately from the variation between PSU totals when the first-stage sampling fraction is small. As shown in Kalton (1983, Chapter 5), the unbiased variance estimator for a simple two-stage selection design consists of a component from each of the two stages, but the term for the second-stage component is multiplied by the first-stage sampling fraction. Therefore, the second-stage contribution becomes negligible as the first-stage sampling fraction decreases. This shortcut procedure based only PSUs is especially convenient in the preparation of complex data files for public use as well as in the analysis of such data, since detailed information on complex design features is not required except for the first-stage sampling.

If the BRR technique is to be applied to other than the paired selection designs, it is necessary to modify the data structure to conform to the technique. In many multistage surveys, stratification is carried out to a maximum and only one PSU is selected from each stratum. In such cases, PSUs can be paired to form collapsed strata to apply the BRR method. This procedure generally leads to some overestimation of the variance because some of the between-strata variability is now included in the within-stratum calculation. The problem is not serious for the case of linear statistics if the collapsing is carried out judiciously; however, the collapsing is generally not recommended for estimating the variance of nonlinear statistics (see Wolter, 1985: 48). The Taylor series approximation method discussed later may be used for the nonlinear statistics. Although not used widely, there is a method of constructing orthogonal balancing for 3 PSUs per stratum (Gurney and Jewett, 1975).

Now let us apply the BRR technique to the 1984 GSS. As introduced in the previous chapter, it used a multistage selection design. The first-stage sampling consisted of selecting one PSU from each of 84 strata of counties or county groups. The first 16 strata were large metropolitan areas and designated as self-representing (or automatically included in the sample). To use the BRR technique, the 84 strata are collapsed into 42 pairs of pseudo-strata. Since the numbering of non-self-representing PSUs in the data file followed approximately the geographic ordering of strata, pairing was done sequentially, based on the PSU code. Thus, the 16 self-representing strata were collapsed into 8 pseudo-strata and the remaining 68 non-self-representing strata into 34 pseudo-strata. But this pairing of the self-representing strata improperly includes variability among them. So, to exclude this and include only the variability within each of the self-representing strata, the combined observations within each self-representing pseudo-stratum were randomly grouped into two pseudo-PSUs.

30

TABLE 4.2
Orthogonal Matrix of Order 44

Rows	Columns (44)
1	11111111111111111111111111111111111111111111
2	10100010100111011110001011100000100011010110
3	10010010010011101111100010111000001000110101
4	11001001010011101111100010111000001000110101
5	11100100101001101111100010111000001000110101
6	10110010010100111011111000101110000010001101
7	11011001001010011011111000101110000010001101
8	10101100100101001110111110001011100000100011
9	11010110010010100111011111000101110000010001
10	11101011001001010011011111000101110000010001
11	10110101100100101001110111110001011100000100
12	10011010110010010100111011111000101110000010
13	10001101011001001010011101111100010111000001
14	11000110101100100101001110111110001011100000
15	10100011010110010010100111011111000101110000
16	10010001101011001001010011101111100010111000
17	10001000110101100100101001110111110001011100
18	10000100011010110010010100111011110001011100
19	10000010001101011001001010011101111100010111
20	11000001000110101100100101001110111110001011
21	11100000100011010110010010100111011111000101
22	11110000010001101011001001010011101111100010
23	10111000001000110101100100101001110111110001
24	11011100000100011010110010010100111011111000
25	10101110000010001101011001001010011101111100
26	10010111000000100011010110010010100111011110
27	10001011100000100011010110010010100111011111
28	11000101110000010001101011001001010011101111
29	11100001011100000100011010110010010100111011
30	11110000101110000010001101011001001010100111011
31	11111000101110000010001101011001001010100111011
32	11111100010111000001000110101100100101001110
33	10111110001011100000100011010110010010100111
34	11011111000101110000010001101011001001010011
35	11101111100010111000001000110101100100101001
36	11110111110001011100000100011010110010010100
37	10111011111000101110000010001101011001001010
38	10011101111100010111000001000110101100100101
39	11001110111110001011100000100011010110010010
40	10100111011111000101110000010001101011001001
41	11010011101111100010111000001000110101001001
42	10101001011011111000101110000010001101011001010
43	10010100110111110001011100000100011010110010
44	11001010011101111100010111000001000110101100

Source: Adapted by permission of the publisher from Wolter (1985), p. 328.

To balance the half-sample replicates to be generated from the 42 pseudo-strata, an orthogonal matrix of order 44 (see Table 4.2) was used, which is filled with zeroes and ones. To match with the 42 strata, the first two columns were dropped (i.e., 44 rows for replicates and 42 columns for pseudo-strata). A zero indicates the inclusion of the first PSU from the strata and a one denotes the inclusion of the second PSU. The rows are the replicates and the columns represent the strata. For example, the first replicate contains the second PSU from each of the 42 pseudo-strata (since all the elements in the first row are ones). Using the rows of the orthogonal matrix, 44 replicates and 44 complement replicates were created.

To estimate the variance of a statistic from the full sample, we needed first to calculate the statistic of interest from each of the 44 replicates and complement replicates. In calculating the replicate estimates, the adjusted sample weights were used. Table 4.3 shows the estimates of the proportion of adults approving the "hitting" for the 44 replicates and their complement replicates. The overall proportion was 60.0 percent. The sampling variance of the overall proportion, estimated by equation 4.3 is 0.000231. Comparing this with the sampling variance of the proportion under the SRS design, $pq/(n-1)=0.000163$ (ignoring the finite population correction), the design effect is 1.42, indicating that the variance of the estimated proportion from the GSS is 42 percent larger than the variance calculated from a simple random sample of the same size. The variance by equation 4.4 also gives similar estimates.

In summary, the BRR technique uses a pseudo-replication procedure to estimate sampling variance and is primarily designed for a paired selection design. It can also be applied to a complex survey which selects one PSU per stratum by pairing strata, but the pairing must be performed judiciously, taking into account the actual sample selection procedure. This technique, however, can require a relatively large amount of time when there are many strata and when the calculation of a statistic requires a great deal of computation, such as in a regression analysis.

Jackknife Repeated Replication

The idea of jackknifing was introduced by Quenouille (1949) as a nonparametric procedure to estimate bias, and later Tukey (1958) suggested how that same procedure could be used to estimate variance. It

TABLE 4.3
Estimated Proportions Approving One Adult Hitting Another in the
BRR Replicates: General Social Survey, 1984 (n = 1,473)

Replicate Number	Estimate (percent) Replicate	Complement	Replicate Number	Estimate (percent) Replicate	Complement
1	60.9	59.2	23	61.4	58.6
2	60.1	59.9	24	57.7	62.4
3	62.1	57.9	25	60.4	59.6
4	58.5	61.7	26	61.7	58.2
5	59.0	61.0	27	59.3	60.6
6	59.8	60.2	28	62.4	57.6
7	58.5	61.5	29	61.0	58.9
8	59.0	61.0	30	61.2	58.7
9	61.3	58.8	31	60.9	59.1
10	59.2	60.8	32	61.6	58.5
11	61.7	58.3	33	61.8	58.2
12	60.2	59.8	34	60.6	59.4
13	62.1	57.8	35	58.6	61.5
14	59.7	60.4	36	59.4	60.7
15	58.1	62.0	37	59.8	60.3
16	56.0	64.2	38	62.0	58.1
17	59.8	60.3	39	58.1	61.9
18	58.6	61.3	40	59.6	60.5
19	58.9	61.1	41	58.8	61.2
20	60.8	59.3	42	59.2	60.8
21	63.4	56.5	43	58.7	61.4
22	58.3	61.7	44	60.5	59.5

Overall estimate = 60.0

Variance estimates:	Variance	Standard Error	Design Effect
by equation 4.3	0.000231	0.0152	1.42
by equation 4.4	0.000227	0.0151	1.40

was first applied in sample surveys by Durbin (1959) in his pioneering work on ratio estimation. Later it was applied to computation of variance in complex surveys by Frankel (1971) in the same manner as the BRR method and named the jackknife repeated replication (JRR). As in BRR, the JRR technique is generally applied to PSUs within strata.

The basic principle of jackknifing can be illustrated by estimating sampling variance of the sample mean from a simple random sample. Suppose n = 5 and sample values of y are 3, 5, 2, 1, and 4. The sample mean then is $\bar{y}$ = 3, and its sampling variance, ignoring the fpc, is

$$v(\bar{y}) = (1/n) \sum (y_i - \bar{y})^2/(n-1) = 0.5. \qquad [4.5]$$

The jackknife variance of the mean is obtained as follows:

1. Compute a pseudo sample mean deleting the first sample value, which results in $\bar{y}_{(1)} = (5+2+1+4)/4 = 12/4$. Now, by deleting the second sample value instead, we obtain the second pseudo mean $\bar{y}_{(2)} = 10/4$; likewise $\bar{y}_{(3)} = 13/4, \bar{y}_{(4)} = 14/4$ and $\bar{y}_{(5)} = 11/4$.
2. Compute the mean of the five pseudo-values $\bar{\bar{y}} = \sum \bar{y}_{(i)}/n = [60/4]/5 = 3$ which is the same as the sample mean.
3. The variance can then be estimated from the variability among the five pseudo-values,

$$v(\bar{y}) = [(n-1)/n] \sum (\bar{y}_{(i)} - \bar{\bar{y}})^2 = 0.5, \qquad [4.6]$$

which gives the same result as equation 4.5.

The replication-based procedures (BRR and JRR) have a distinct advantage: they can be applied to estimators that are not expressible in terms of formulas, such as the sample median, as well as to formula-based estimators. No elementary textbook gives a formula for calculating the sampling variance of the median, but the jackknife procedure can offer an estimate. Using the same example as above, the sample median is 3 and the five pseudo-medians are 3, 2.5, 3.5, 3.5, and 2.5 (the mean of these pseudo-medians is 3). The variance of the median is estimated as 0.8, using equation 4.6.

In the same manner, the jackknife procedure can also be applied to replicated sampling. We can remove replicates one at a time and compute pseudo-values to estimate the jackknife variance, although this does not offer any computational advantage in this case. But it can also be applied to any random groups that are formed from any probability sample. For instance, a systematic sample can be divided into random or systematic subgroups for the jackknife procedure. For other sample designs, random groups can be formed following the practical rules suggested by Wolter (1985: 31-33). The basic idea is to form random groups in such a way that each random group has the same sample design as the parent sample. This requires detailed information on the actual sample design, but unfortunately such information is usually not available in most public use survey data files. The jackknife procedure is, therefore, applied usually to PSUs rather than to random groups.

A replicate in a paired selection design is formed by removing one PSU from a stratum and weighting the remaining PSU in that stratum to retain the stratum's proportion in the total sample. The complement replicate is formed in the same manner by exchanging the removed and retained PSU in the stratum. A pseudo-value is estimated from each replicate. For a weighted sample, the sample weights in the retained PSU need to be inflated to account for the observations in the removed PSU. The inflated weight is obtained by dividing the sum of the weights in the retained PSU by a factor $(1 - w_d/w_t)$, where w_d is the sum of weights in the deleted PSU and w_t is the sum of weights in all the PSUs in that stratum. The factor represents the complement of the deleted PSU's proportion of the total stratum weight. Then the variance of a sample statistic in a paired selection design calculated from the full sample can be estimated from pseudo-values u'_h and complement pseudo-values u''_h in stratum h by

$$\mathrm{v}(\bar{u}) = \sum [(u'_h - \bar{u})^2 + (u''_h - \bar{u})^2]/2 = \sum (u'_h - u''_h)^2/4. \quad [4.7]$$

This estimator has the same form as equation 4.3 and can be modified to include one replicate, without averaging with the complement from each stratum as in equation 4.4 for the BRR method, which gives

$$\mathrm{v}^*(\bar{u}) = \sum (u'_h - \bar{u})^2. \quad [4.8]$$

The JRR is not restricted to a paired selection design but is applicable to any number of PSUs per stratum. If we let u_{hi} be the estimate of U from the h-th stratum and i-th replicate, n_h be the number of sampled PSUs in the h-th stratum, and r_h be the number of replicates formed in stratum h, then the variance is estimated by

$$\mathrm{v}(\bar{u}) = \sum_h^L (n_h - 1)/r_h \sum_i^{r_h} (u_{hi} - \bar{u})^2. \quad [4.9]$$

If each of the PSUs in stratum h is removed to form a replicate, $r_h = n_h$ in each stratum. But the formation of n_h replicates in h-th stratum is not required. When the number of strata is large and n_h is two or more, the computation can be reduced by using only one replicate in each stratum. However, a sufficient number of replicates must be used in analytic studies to ensure adequate degrees of freedom.

Table 4.4 shows the results of applying the JRR technique to the collapsed paired design of the 1984 GSS used in the BRR computation. The estimated proportions of adults approving "the hitting of other adults" are shown for the 42 jackknife replicates and their complements. Applying equation 4.7, we obtain a variance estimate of 0.000238 with a design effect of 1.46, and these are about the same as those obtained by the BRR technique. Using only the 42 replicates and excluding the complements (equation 4.8), we obtain a variance estimate of 0.000275 with a design effect of 1.68.

From a closer examination of data in Table 4.4, one may get an impression that there is less variation among the JRR replicate estimates compared with the BRR replicate estimates in Table 4.3. But we should note that the JRR represents a different strategy that uses a different method to estimate the variance. Note that equation 4.3 for the BRR includes the number of replicates (t) in the denominator, while equation 4.7 for the JRR is not dependent on the number of replicates. The reason is that in the JRR the replicate estimates themselves are dependent on the number of replicates formed. Since the replicate is formed by deleting one unit, the replicate estimate would be closer to the overall estimate when a large number of units are available to form the replicates, compared to the situation where a small number of units are used. Therefore, there is no reason to include the number of replicates in equations 4.7 and 4.8. However, the number of replicates needs to be taken into account when the number of replicates used is smaller than the total number of PSUs, as in equation 4.9.

In summary, the JRR technique is based on a pseudo-replication method and can estimate sampling variances from complex sample surveys. No restrictions on the sample selection design are needed, but forming replicates requires considerable care and must take into account the sampling design of the parent sample. Modification of the original data structure cannot be done in an arbitrary fashion, but must adhere to the design of the parent sample. As noted, this detailed design information is seldom available to secondary data analysts. For instance, if more information on ultimate clusters had been available in the GSS data file, we could have formed more convincing random groups adhering more closely to actual sample design rather than applying the JRR technique to a collapsed paired design.

Closely related to the jackknife is the bootstrap method popularized by Efron (1979). The basic idea is to emulate the selection of samples from a population created by replicating each observation in

TABLE 4.4

Estimated Proportions Approving One Adult Hitting Another in the
JRR Replicates: General Social Survey, 1984 ($n = 1,473$)

Replicate Number	Estimate (percent)		Replicate Number	Estimate (percent)	
	Replicate	Complement		Replicate	Complement
1	60.2	59.8	22	60.3	60.0
2	60.2	59.8	23	60.0	60.0
3	60.0	60.0	24	60.4	59.6
4	60.3	59.8	25	60.1	59.8
5	60.0	60.1	26	59.8	60.3
6	59.9	60.1	27	59.9	60.1
7	60.0	60.0	28	60.1	60.0
8	60.0	60.0	29	59.5	60.3
9	59.9	60.2	30	59.9	60.1
10	60.1	60.0	31	59.6	60.2
11	59.8	60.2	32	60.5	59.6
12	59.9	60.1	33	60.1	59.9
13	59.8	60.2	34	60.3	59.8
14	60.0	60.1	35	60.1	59.8
15	59.6	60.5	36	60.2	59.8
16	60.4	59.6	37	60.0	60.0
17	59.9	60.0	38	59.6	60.4
18	59.8	60.2	39	59.9	60.1
19	59.8	60.2	40	60.5	59.6
20	59.9	60.1	41	60.4	59.8
21	60.0	60.0	42	60.7	59.4

Overall estimate = 60.0

Variance estimates:	Variance	Standard Error	Design Effect
by equation 4.7	0.000238	0.0154	1.46
by equation 4.8	0.000275	0.0166	1.68

the original sample many times, say, 100,000 times. We then estimate the variance from the repeated bootstrap samples, drawn, for example, 10,000 times. The idea is consistent with pseudo-replication, and there is no reason that it cannot be applied to complex surveys. However, the standard bootstrap method may require certain modifications before being applied to a finite population situation. For example, Chao and Lo (1985) suggested duplicating each observation in the host sample only N/n times to create the bootstrap population for simple random sampling without replacement. For sampling plans with unequal probability of selection, the replication of the observations needs to be in proportion to the sample weight, that is, the bootstrap sample should be selected using the PPS procedure. These options and the possible effects of deviating from the fundamental assumption of independent and identically distributed samples have not been thoroughly investigated.

Though promising for many statistical problems, the bootstrap method appears less practical than jackknifing for estimating the variance in complex surveys. Bootstrapping is more time-consuming and expensive than jackknifing. As Tukey (1986) puts it, "For the moment, jackknifery seems the most nearly realistic approach to assessing many of the sources of uncertainty" when compared with bootstrapping and other methods.

The Taylor Series Method

The Taylor series expansion has been used in a variety of situations in mathematics and statistics. One early application of the series expansion was to obtain an approximation to the value of functions that are hard to calculate, for example, the exponential e^x or logarithmic ($\log(x)$) function. This application was in the days before calculators had special function keys or when we did not have access to the appropriate tables. The Taylor series expansion for e^x involves taking the first and higher order derivatives of e^x with respect to x, evaluating the derivatives at some value, usually zero, and building up a series of terms based on the derivatives. The expansion for e^x is

$$1 + x + x^2/2! + x^3/3! + x^4/4! + \ldots$$

This is a specific application of the following general formula expanded at a:

$$f(x) = f(a) + f'(a)(x - a) + f''(a)(x - a)^2/2! + f'''(a)(x - a)^3/3! + \ldots$$

In statistics, the Taylor series is used to obtain an approximation to some nonlinear function, and then the variance of the function is based on the Taylor series approximation to the function. Often the approximation provides a reasonable estimate to the function, and sometimes the approximation is even a linear function. This idea of variance estimation has several names in the literature, including the linearization method, the delta method (Kalton, 1983: 44) and the propagation of variance (Kish, 1965: 583).

38

In statistical applications, the expansion is evaluated at the mean or expected value of x, written as $E(x)$. If we use $E(x)$ for "a" in the above general expansion formula, we have

$$f(x) = f[E(x)] + f'[E(x)][x - E(x)] + f''[E(x)][x - E(x)]^2/2! + \ldots$$

The variance of $f(x) = E[f^2(x)] - E^2[f(x)]$ by definition, and using the Taylor series expansion, we have

$$V[f(x)] = \{f'[E(x)]\}^2 V(x) + \ldots \qquad [4.10]$$

The same ideas carry over to functions of more than one random variable. In the case of a function of two variances, the Taylor series expansion yields

$$V[f(x_1,x_2)] \doteq (\partial f/\partial x_1)(\partial f/\partial x_2) \, \text{Cov}(x_1,x_2). \qquad [4.11]$$

Applying equation 4.11 to a ratio of two variables x and y, that is $r = y/x$, we obtain the variance formula for a ratio estimator

$$V(r) = [V(y) + r^2 V(x) - 2r \, \text{Cov}(x,y)] /x^2 + \ldots$$

$$= r^2 [V(y)/y^2 + V(x)/x^2 - 2 \, \text{Cov}(x,y)/xy] + \ldots$$

Extending equation 4.11 to the case of c random variables, the approximate variance of $\theta = f(x_1,x_2,\ldots,x_c)$ is

$$V(\theta) \doteq \sum \sum (\partial f/\partial x_i)(\partial f/\partial x_j) \, \text{Cov}(x_i,x_j). \qquad [4.12]$$

Applying equation 4.12 to a weighted estimator

$$(f(Y) = \hat{Y}_i = \sum w_j y_{ij}, j = 1, \ldots, c)$$

involving c variables in a sample of n observations, Woodruff (1971) showed that

$$V(\theta) \doteq V[\sum w_i \sum (\partial f/\partial y_j) y_{ij}]. \qquad [4.13]$$

This alternative form of the linearized variance of nonlinear estimator offers computational advantages since it bypasses the computation of the $c \times c$ covariance matrix in equation 4.12. This convenience of converting a multistage estimation problem into a univariate problem is realized by a simple interchange of summations. This general computational procedure can be applied to a variety of nonlinear estimators including regression coefficients (Fuller, 1975; Tepping, 1968).

TABLE 4.5

Standard Errors Estimated by Taylor Series Method for Percent
Approving One Adult Hitting Another by Gender, Race, and
Education: General Social Survey, 1984 (n = 1,473)

	Subgroup	Estimate (percent)	Standard Error (percent)	Design Effect
	Overall	60.0	1.52	1.41
Gender	Male	63.5	2.29	1.58
	Female	56.8	1.96	1.21
Race	White	63.3	1.61	1.43
	Nonwhite	39.1	3.93	1.30
Education	Some college	68.7	2.80	1.06
	High School grad.	63.3	2.14	1.55
	All others	46.8	2.85	1.27

For a complex survey, this method of approximation is applied to
the PSU totals within the stratum. That is, the variance estimate is a
weighted combination of the variation in equation 4.13 across PSUs
within the same stratum. These formulas are complex but can require
much less computing time than the replication-based methods discussed in the previous sections. This method can be applied to any
statistic that is expressed mathematically, for example, the mean, the
regression coefficient, but not to such nonfunctional statistics as the
median and other percentiles.

We now return to the GSS example of estimating the variance of
sample proportions. Table 4.5 shows the results of applying the Taylor series method to the proportion of adults approving the hitting of
other adults by gender, race, and level of education. The proportion is
computed as a ratio of weighted sum of all positive responses to the
sum of all the weights. Its standard error is computed applying equation 4.13 modified to include the PSUs and strata. The design effect
for the overall proportion is 1.41, which is about the same as those estimated by using the other two methods whose results are shown in
Tables 4.3 and 4.4. The estimated proportion varies by gender, race,
and the level of education. Since the subgroup sizes are small, the
standard errors for the subgroups are larger than that for the overall
estimate. Also, the design effects for subgroup proportions are different from that for the overall estimate. This example shows that the de-

sign effects for subgroups do differ from the design effects for the total group and other variables, and it is safer, but more costly, to estimate anew each analysis. More is said on this topic in the second section of the next chapter.

5. PREPARING FOR SURVEY DATA ANALYSIS

The preceding chapters have concentrated on the complex nature of survey designs and techniques for variance estimation for these designs. Before applying the sample weights and the methods for assessing the design effect, one should consider the data requirements for the estimation of the statistics and their variances using the existing software. These requirements are somewhat more stringent for complex survey data than for data from an SRS because of the weights and the design effect considerations.

Importance of Preliminary Analysis

Survey data analysis begins with a preliminary exploration to see whether the data are suitable for a meaningful analysis. One important consideration in the preliminary examination of a secondary data source is whether there are a sufficient number of observations available in the various subgroups to support the proposed analysis. Based on the unweighted tabulations, the analyst determines whether the sample sizes are large enough and whether categories of the variables should be grouped. The tabulations also give the number of the observations with missing values and those with extreme values, which could indicate either measurement errors or errors of transcription.

The analyst must pay attention to the case selection and exclusion procedures and their effect on the sample weights. For instance, selecting only persons 25 years of age and over for a certain analysis would not alter the basic weights. This selection process simply redefines the analytic domain. But excluding cases because of missing values would alter the original weighting scheme. One method of handling this is to inflate the weights associated with the retained cases to compensate for the excluded cases. When performing this type of adjustment, one is assuming there is no systematic pattern among the subjects with missing values. For example, if all the subjects with missing values were males or all fell into a limited age range, then it would be inappropriate simply to inflate the weight of the remaining cases. No adjustment may be necessary when a very small proportion of cases is excluded, but when the proportion excluded is large, the original weights may be adjusted in a manner similar to that used in nonresponse adjustment. An alternative to inflating the weights is to impute the missing value by some reasonable estimator. However, imputation is not necessarily a better solution.

Prior to any substantive analysis incorporating the design, it is also necessary to tabulate the unweighted data to see whether all the PSUs have a sufficient number of observations. It is possible that some PSUs may contain only a few observations, or even none, because of nonresponse and the case selection procedures applied. One way of dealing with PSUs with no observations is to combine PSUs and strata in a way that reflects the design as much as possible. The PSUs with none or only a few observations may be combined with an adjacent PSU within the same stratum. The stratum with a single PSU as a result of combining PSUs may then be combined with an adjacent stratum. However, collapsing too many PSUs destroys the original sample design. The resulting data analysis may be of questionable value, since it is no longer possible to determine what population is represented by the sample resulting from the combination of the PSUs and strata. The number of observations that is needed in each PSU is dependent on the type of analysis planned. The required number would be larger for analytic studies than for estimation of descriptive statistics. A general guideline is that the number should be large enough to estimate the intra-PSU variance for the given estimate.

To illustrate this point, we consider the GSS data. An unweighted tabulation by stratum and PSU showed that the number of observations in the PSUs ranged from 8 to 49 with most of the frequencies being larger than 13, indicating that the PSUs are probably large enough for estimating variances for means and proportions. For an analytic study, we may want to investigate the percent of adults approving of hitting, by education and gender. For this analysis we need to determine if there are a number of PSUs without observations in a particular education by gender category. If there are many PSUs with no observations for some education by gender category, it calls into question the estimation of the variance-covariance matrix, which is based on the variation in the PSU totals within the strata. The education (3 levels) by gender (2 levels) tabulation by PSU showed that 42 of the 84 PSUs had at least one gender by education cell with no observations. Even after collapsing education into two categories, we would have to combine nearly one-half of the PSUs. Therefore, we should not attempt to investigate simultaneously the gender and education variables in relation to the question about hitting. However, it is possible to analyze gender or education alone in relation to hitting without combining many PSUs and strata.

The next step in a preliminary analysis would be to compute the summary statistics and to explore the basic distributions of key variables, both unweighted and weighted. The unweighted tabulations may point out the need for refining operational definitions of variables and for combining categories of certain variables. In constructing composite variables based on combination of a number of separate data items, one needs to examine both the unweighted and weighted tabulations of each item. Based on the weighted statistics, one may learn about interesting patterns and distributions of certain variables in the population. However, we cannot assess the statistical precision of the estimates because we have not yet taken into account the data structure in the variance estimation.

After analyzing the variables one at a time, we can next examine variables for relationships with one another. A preliminary investigation of the existence of relations can be performed using standard SRS-based procedures. The SRS-based tests can be used to screen out variables that are clearly not related to one another or to some dependent variable. This screening analysis is often performed because the analyses that incorporate both the sample weights and the data structure are much more computer intensive than the SRS-based procedures. In relational analyses, one rule of thumb is to drop from further consideration any variable that is not significant at an α level of 0.15. The value of 0.15 for the probability of Type I error is suggested because it guards against situations with a design effect less than one. Those variables found to be significant need to be examined further by taking the data structure into account.

In summary, one should first obtain unweighted tabulations to see whether enough cases are available and they are distributed across the PSUs in a way that allows for a meaningful analysis. Next, perform the planned analyses using the sample weights to discover meaningful patterns. The SRS-based statistical tests are used to help select the variables for further consideration. This approach reduces the number of variables that must be considered when the data structure is considered. Reduction of the number of variables is suggested because the procedures for incorporating the data structure require much more computer time than the SRS-based procedures, which incorporate only the sample weights.

Choices of the Method for Variance Estimation

Incorporating the design features into the analysis requires choosing a special method of variance estimation. As discussed in Chapter 4, there are three variance estimation methods—BRR, JRR, and the Taylor series approximation—that are used in practice. Before discussing which one to use, we present a method that can be used in simple analytic studies. It utilizes the design effect obtained from direct estimates of variance for similar variables in the same data source or from the same variable in other similarly designed surveys. It is not possible to apply this method when such estimates from previous analyses are not available.

We shall use data from the 1984 GSS to demonstrate the application of this approach. The weighted estimate of the proportion of adults who were ever threatened by a gun is 19.7 percent with a standard of error of 1.04 based on the simple random sampling assumption. Applying the design effect of 1.41 obtained by the Taylor series approximation for the percentage of adult approving "hitting" (see Table 4.5), we can obtain a standard error of 1.23 percent. This estimate results from the multiplication of the SRS standard error of 1.04 percent by the square root of the design effect, $\sqrt{1.41}$. The 95 percent confidence limits for this percentage can then be estimated as 19.7 ± (1.96 × 1.23) where 1.96 is the value from the standard normal tables.

The same logic can be used in a significance test using a t or z statistic. Multiplying the variance by the design effect allows one to recalculate the test statistic and to reassess the significance level. Though simple, this method cannot substitute for a direct estimation of variance since the true design effect for a variable cannot always be predicted well from that of other variables.

It is interesting to compare the above approximate confidence limit with the confidence interval resulting from a direct estimation of the standard error for the percentage of those who were ever threatened by someone with a gun. The direct estimation of the standard error is 0.92 which yields a design effect of 0.78, indicating that the actual confidence interval should have been considerably shorter than that shown above. The situation may be different for another variable.

From the same data source, 42.4 percent of adults felt that medical care is the government's responsibility, with a standard error of 1.75 percent and a design effect of 1.84. For this case, the use of 1.41 as the design effect would have been an underestimate. It is often recommended that the design effect be averaged over several related variables instead of basing the estimate of the design effect on a single variable. However, even under the best of circumstances, this indirect procedure should be considered as a provisional measure, and it cannot completely replace a direct estimation of variance. Moreover, this approach generally does not work for a multivariate analysis where the covariance structure is required.

For a direct estimation of variance, we use either BRR, JRR, or the Taylor series approximation. These three general methods have been evaluated empirically by several researchers (Bean, 1975; Frankel, 1971; Kish and Frankel, 1974; Lemeshow and Levy, 1979), and Krewski and Rao (1981) have performed some theoretical comparisons of these approaches. These evaluation studies tend to show that none of the three methods perform consistently better or worse, and that the choice may depend in most cases on the relative costs of computing and the availability of software. In a few cases, the choice may depend on the type of statistic to be estimated or the sample design used.

In terms of computing time, the formula-based Taylor series approximation can be preferable to the replication-based methods (BRR and JRR), but it depends on the particular programs that are used. When the number of PSUs is large, the difference in computing times can be considerable. However, as discussed in Chapter 4, the Taylor series method is not applicable for the median or other percentiles and nonparametric statistics. The replication-based methods are more general and can be applied with these statistics.

The BRR method is designed for a paired selection design. When one PSU is selected from each stratum, the PSUs must be paired to create pseudo-strata in order to apply the BRR method. When more than two PSUs are selected from each stratum, it is difficult to create a paired design, and it is better to use the JRR or the Taylor series method.

In practice, the choice of method is limited since only a few programs are available at the present time and software is not available for all the statistical methods currently favored by the analysts. The available programs will be reviewed in the last section of this chapter.

Data Requirements for Weights and the Design Effect

As discussed in Chapter 3, the weight and the design effect are basic ingredients needed for a complete analysis of survey data. In extracting data items from a secondary source, it is necessary to include the weights and the identification of sampling units and strata. Since these data items are labeled differently in various survey data sources, it is important to read the documentation or consult with the source agency or person to understand the survey design and the data preparation procedures.

The weights are usually available in major survey data sources. As noted earlier, the weights reflect the selection probabilities and the adjustments for nonresponse and poststratification. The weights are generally expressed as expansion weights, and in certain analyses it may be more convenient to convert them into the relative weights. For some surveys (e.g., the GSS), the weights are not explicitly labeled as such and it is necessary to study the sample design to realize that the weight must be derived from the number of adults in the household. It may also be necessary to perform poststratification adjustments to make the demographic composition of the sample comparable to the population. If the weights are not available even after contacting the provider of the data, we may choose not to use the data or to assume a self-weighting sample, but this assumption could be wrong, leading to possibly biased conclusions.

The calculation of the design effect requires information on the first-stage selection procedure, that is, the identification of strata and PSUs. If one PSU is selected from each stratum, as in the GSS, the stratum identification is the same as the PSU identification. If stratification is not used or the stratum identification is not available from the data, one can perform the analysis assuming an unrestricted cluster sampling. If there is no information on the stratum and PSU, an analysis of the data may be performed based on the SRS assumption. However, it is important to investigate whether such an assumption is reasonable for the given sample design.

When stratification is used and the stratum identification is available, we need to make sure that at least two PSUs are available in each stratum. Otherwise, it is not possible to estimate the variance. If only one cluster is selected from each stratum, it is necessary to pair the strata to form pseudo-strata. Pairing the strata requires a good understanding of the sample design. An example of a particular strategy for pairing, using the GSS, was presented in Chapter 3. In the absence of any useful information from the data document, a random pairing may be acceptable. Stanek and Lemeshow (1977) have investigated the effect of pairing based on the National Health Examination Survey and found that variance estimates for the weighted mean and combined ratio estimate were insensitive to different pairings of the strata, but this conclusion may not apply to all surveys.

Available Computing Resources

This review of software describes the major programs available and used extensively. One set of programs that have been around for over ten years is the SUDAAN package, which is available from the Research Triangle Institute. It uses the Taylor series method to estimate variances and covariances and was developed to be compatible with SAS (Statistical Analysis System) for mainframe computers. One procedure, SESUDAAN (Shah, 1980), is used to estimate the variance for rates, means, totals, or for the difference of these statistics. The SURREGR procedure (Holt, 1977) is used for regression and related analyses. Recently, a procedure for logistic regression has been added. The SAS user may find these procedures easy to implement, but it may be difficult to read the program documentation and the output without help from an experienced user.

The WESVAR program computes basic survey estimates (descriptive statistics) and their associated sampling errors, using either BRR or JRR. It was developed as an SAS procedure for mainframe computers and is available from Westat, Inc. (Flyer and Mohadjer, 1988). It requires that each record in the input data file contain the replicate weights in addition to the weight for the full sample. The procedure NASSREG performs regression analyses. A new procedure recently added to this package is NASSLOG, which fits a logistic regression model using the BRR method. The program documentation is easy to understand for SAS users, but new users may need some instruction in preparing the replicate weights before using the procedure.

CARP is a FORTRAN program for computing descriptive statistics and their estimated sampling errors, as well as performing regression analysis using the Taylor series method. It is available from the Statistical Laboratory at Iowa State University. The original version for mainframe computers is known as SUPER CARP (Hidiroglou et al., 1980) and a shorter version of this program is available as MINI CARP. These programs contain a number of options for different sampling designs, including PSUs with and without replacement, stratum sampling ratios, and different error structure problems. The program documentation is good and especially useful to the more statistically inclined users.

PC CARP is a microcomputer version of the CARP (Fuller et al., 1986). It is designed for the IBM PC and compatibles with at least 450K of memory and a Math Co-Processor. It is menu driven, and most menu requests are self-explanatory for those who are familiar with basic concepts and methods described in the first four chapters of this book. The program documentation is easy to understand with examples showing the computer screens.

There are programs available in other computing environments, including OSIRIS, which contains the PSALMS procedure for descriptive statistics and the REPERR procedure for regression analysis. Additionally several government statistical agencies have developed some special purpose programs. There are also other programs written for some special survey projects such as the World Fertility Survey.

Four of these procedures for regression analysis (SURREGR, SUPER CARP, REPERR, and NASSREG) have been extensively evaluated by Cohen et al. (1988) using data from the National Medical Care Expenditure Survey. Based on a comparison of computational efficiency and analytical flexibility, they selected the SURREGR procedure as the recommended program of choice. Specifically, they noted that the SURREGR procedure required the minimum number of programming statements and the least amount of CPU time.

There are two other programs of interest for conducting discrete multivariate analysis. One of these, CPLX, analyzes categorical data by fitting log-linear models using either a modified jackknife method or BRR. A mainframe version is available from the Bureau of the Census (Fay, 1983), and a version for the PC is under development. CPLX is similar to the program ECTA (used to analyze log-linear models for SRS data) in the specification of the model, but it requires extensive manipulation of the input data to create the different replicates used by the jackknife method or BRR in the analysis. It is possible to create the replicates by using CROSSTABS in SPSS or SUMMARY in SAS and to pass them directly to CPLX. The documentation is fairly difficult for new users.

CATMOD is a procedure in SAS that enables users to perform analyses of a categorical dependent variable using the weighted least squares approach to the analysis of contingency data developed by Grizzle et al. (1969). The user first estimates the variance-covariance matrix for proportions in a contingency table by using either the BRR, JRR or Taylor series method. This matrix, along with the proportions, is then entered directly into CATMOD. As currently implemented, it allows the user to perform a subset of the wide range of analyses possible under the weighted least squares approach.

Detailed illustrations presented in Chapters 6 and 7 were computed by three microcomputer based programs: PC CARP, PC CPLX[3] and CATMOD in PC SAS (SAS Institute, 1985). In addition to these special-purpose programs, the matrix commands in MINITAB (Ryan et al., 1975) were used to perform the weighted least squares analysis of the logit in Chapter 7 and the AVERAGE and REGRESS procedures in BASS (BASS Institute, 1988) were used to perform the preliminary analyses in Chapter 6.

6. CONDUCTING A REGRESSION ANALYSIS

This chapter focuses on the regression analysis of data from a complex survey. The emphasis is on the demonstration of the effects of incorporating the weights and the data structure on the regression results. The discussion of the model is followed by a review of the necessary changes in the methodology to analyze data from a complex survey. An example is presented in which the variables are selected to illustrate the method rather than to present substantive findings.

The Linear Model for Complex Survey Data

Both regression analysis and the analysis of variance examine the linear relation between a continuous dependent variable and a set of independent variables. To test hypotheses, it is assumed that the dependent variable follows a normal distribution. The following equation shows the type of relation being considered by these methods for $i = 1, 2, \ldots, n$.

$$Y_i = X_0 \beta_0 + X_{1i} \beta_1 + X_{2i} \beta_2 + \ldots + X_{pi} \beta_p + \varepsilon_i \quad [6.1]$$

This is a linear model in the sense that the dependent variable, Y_i, is represented by a linear combination of the β_j's plus ε_i. The independent variables, the X_j's, may involve square terms, logarithms or other transformations. The β_j is the coefficient of the X_j's variable in the equation and ε_i is the random error term in the model that is assumed to follow a normal distribution with a mean of 0 and a constant variance and to be independent of the other error terms.

In regression analysis, the independent variables are continuous variables, and the β_j's are the corresponding coefficients. In the ANOVA, the independent variables (X_j's) are indicator variables (each category of a factor has a separate indicator variable coded 1 or 0) that show which effects are added to the model, and the β_j's are the effects. The situation with both continuous and discrete independent variables can also be treated, and the analysis of covariance is one example of this. Another example is multiple-classification analysis (Andrew et al., 1973), in which case the coefficients for indicator variables are expressed as the deviations from the overall mean of the dependent variable after adjusting for other indicator and continuous variables considered. There is no real change in the methodology to deal with these different situations; the only differences are in the interpretation of the β_j's and the role played by the X_{ji}'s.

Ordinary least squares (OLS) estimation is used to obtain estimates of the regression coefficients or the effects in the linear model when the data result from a SRS. However, several changes in the methodology are required to deal with data from a complex sample. The data now consist of the individual observations plus the sample weights and the design descriptors. As was discussed in Chapter 2, the subjects from a complex sample usually have different probabilities of selection. In addition, in a complex survey the random error terms are often no longer independent of one another because of features of the sample design. Because of these departures from SRS, the OLS estimates of the model parameters and their variances are biased. Thus, confidence intervals and tests of hypotheses may be misleading.

Nathan and Holt (1980), Konijn (191962), Holt et al. (1980), Fuller (1975), Shah et al. (1977) and Pfeffermann and Nathan (1981) are among a number of authors who have addressed these issues. They do not concur on a single approach to the analysis, but they all agree that the use of OLS as the estimation methodology can be inappropriate. Rather than provide a review of all these articles, the focus here is on an approach that covers the widest range of situations and that also has software available and widely disseminated. This approach to the estimation of the model parameters is the weighted least squares (WLS), and its use is supported by the work of Fuller (1975), Holt et al. (1980) and Shah et al. (1977).

The weight in the WLS method is the inverse of the probability of selection, the simple expansion weight, or it can also be the weight adjusted for nonresponse and poststratification. This weight takes into account that a subject with a small probability of selection represents more people in the population than does a subject with a larger probability of selection. The use of the weights in this fashion is consistent with what one does in estimating the mean of a stratified sample as was discussed in Chapter 3.

While the use of the WLS approach for the estimation of the parameters deals with the unequal probability of selection, it does not account for the possible correlation between the error terms and their effect on the variance estimation. For example, when household is the PSU and several individuals in the household are sampled, the individual responses would be highly correlated and, hence, the error terms would be correlated. Another example of correlated error terms would be when the classroom is the PSU and students from the class are the units of analysis. If students' attitudes about a school issue are measured, they may be correlated because of exposure to the same teacher.

The correlation of the error terms has a minimal effect on the estimation of the parameters and can be safely ignored. However, it must be dealt with relative to the variance and covariance of the estimated parameters.[4] To account for this correlation as well as the other complexities introduced by the sample design and other adjustments to the weights, one of the three methods (BRR, JRR, or Taylor series) discussed in Chapter 4 may be used in the estimation of the variance-covariance or dispersion matrix of the estimates of the model parameters. Since these methods use the PSU total rather than the individual value as the basis for the variance computation, the degrees of freedom for this design equal the number of distinct PSUs minus the number of strata, instead of the number of individuals in the sample. The degrees of freedom associated with the sum of squares for error are then the number of PSUs minus the number of strata minus the number of terms in the model.

An Example of Regression Analysis from NHANES II

This example uses data from the NHANES II (the second National Health and Nutrition Examination Survey) conducted in 1976-1980 by the National Center for Health Statistics (NCHS). The sample design was a stratified, multistage, probability cluster sample of households. The target population was the civilian noninstitutionalized U.S. population 6 months through 74 years of age. The PSU in NHANES II were counties or small groups of contiguous counties, and the PSUs were grouped into 64 strata, based on health and demographic variables. One PSU was selected from each stratum using a modified control selection technique (Goodman and Kish, 1950). Subsequent hierarchical sampling units included census enumeration districts, clusters of households, and eligible persons. Preschool children, the aged, and the poor were oversampled to provide sufficient numbers of persons in these subgroups. The data collection involved a personal interview and medical examination, including tests and other procedures used in clinical practice (McDowell et al., 1981).

The sample weight contained in the public use data tapes is the expansion weight adjusted for nonresponse and poststratification. Since certain data items were collected from subsamples, several different weights were computed, and the user must choose the appropriate weight for a given analysis. Since one PSU was selected from each stratum, NCHS paired the 64 PSUs based on their locations to form 32 pseudo-strata. The identifications for the pseudo-strata and PSUs are included in the data tapes and no further modification of them is required.

To illustrate a regression analysis, we chose to investigate the body mass index, a measure of obesity, for adults 18 through 74 years of age. The independent variables selected were age, race, sex, marital status, poverty index, education, use of vitamin supplement, and smoking status. From the NHANES II sample we extracted 12,486 adults, excluding 34 persons with missing values for height or body weight. Since the number of observations excluded is so small, we did not readjust the weights. To determine whether there were any problems in the distribution of the data across the PSUs, an unweighted tabulation was performed and showed that the number of observations available in the PSUs ranged from 123 to 324. The expansion weights were divided by an average expansion weight of 11,388.8 to obtain the relative weights. This scaling of the weight was done to reduce the weighted number of observations since many microcomputer-based programs limit the number of observations.

The body mass index was calculated by dividing the body weight (in kilograms) by the square of the height (in meters). Age was measured in years, education was measured as the number of years of schooling, and the poverty index was calculated as a ratio of the family income to the poverty level. Missing values were replaced by the average value of the variable for a small number of cases. The variables mentioned above are continuous variables, whereas the other variables are binary variables coded as follows: race (1=black; 0=nonblack), marital status (1=married; 0=nonmarried), sex (1=male; 0=female), use of vitamin supplement (1=yes; 0=no), and smoking status (1=current smoker; 0=nonsmokers). In addition, the age squared term is included to account for a possible nonlinear effect of age on the body mass index.

To demonstrate that the weight and design effect makes a difference, the analysis was performed under three different options.

1. Unweighted, ignoring the data structure
2. Weighted, ignoring the data structure
3. Weighted, considering the data structure

The first option assumes simple random sampling, and the second recognizes the case weight but ignores the design effect. The third option provides a more appropriate analysis for the given sample design.

Descriptive statistics for the variables selected for the regression analysis are shown in Table 6.1. The first and second analyses shown in this table were performed by the AVERAGE procedure in BASS. For the third analysis, the RATIOS procedure in PC CARP was used since it computes the weighted mean or proportion and its variance incorporating the sample design features. To use RATIOS, it is necessary to create a dummy variable (described as "intercept" in the documentation). The sum of the weighted intercept variable is simply the sum of the weights and is the denominator used in computing the mean or proportion.

The statistics shown in Table 6.1 are means for the continuous variables, proportions for the binary variables, and their standard errors. There are only slight differences between the unweighted and weighted means and proportions except for the mean age. For example, the unweighted mean body mass index (25.37) is slightly higher

TABLE 6.1

Descriptive Statistics for the Variables Selected for Regression
Analysis for Adults 18-74 Years from NHANES II Under Three
Different Analytic Options (n = 12,486)

Analytic Option	Variable	Mean or Proportion	Standard Error	Design Effect*
1. Unweighted, ignoring the data structure:				
	Body mass index	25.37	0.044	—
	Age in years	46.30	0.160	—
	Race (black)	0.114	0.0028	—
	Gender (male)	0.473	0.0045	—
	Marital status (married)	0.655	0.0042	—
	Poverty index	2.59	0.013	—
	Education (yrs. of schooling)	11.31	0.032	—
	Vitamin supplement (yes)	0.363	0.0043	—
	Smoking now (yes)	0.343	0.0042	—
2. Weighted, ignoring the data structure:				
	Body mass index	25.10	0.043	—
	Age in years	41.07	0.144	—
	Race (black)	0.104	0.0027	—
	Gender (male)	0.476	0.0045	—
	Marital status (married)	0.661	0.0042	—
	Poverty index	2.69	0.013	—
	Education (yrs. of schooling)	11.89	0.030	—
	Vitamin supplement (yes)	0.372	0.0043	—
	Smoking now (yes)	0.387	0.0049	—
3. Weighted, considering the data structure:				
	Body mass index	25.10	0.070	2.58
	Age in years	41.07	0.288	4.01
	Race (black)	0.104	0.0126	21.23
	Gender (male)	4.476	0.0042	0.89
	Marital status (married)	0.661	0.0085	3.98
	Poverty index	2.69	0.030	5.50
	Education (yrs. of schooling)	11.89	0.080	7.26
	Vitamin supplement (yes)	0.372	0.0082	3.57
	Smoking now (yes)	0.387	0.0062	2.09

*Square of the ratio of the standard error in (3) to the standard error in (2).

than the weighted mean (25.10). The unweighted proportion of adults taking a vitamin supplement is 36.3 percent, compared to the weighted proportion of 37.2 percent. But the weighted mean age is about 5 years less than the unweighted mean because the elderly were oversampled.

When the data structure is ignored (the first and second options), the standard errors for the weighted and unweighted means or proportions are practically the same. However, when the data structure is taken into account (the third option), the standard errors increase for all variables except gender. This difference is expressed in terms of design effect in the table (the square of the ratio of standard error in the third option to that in the second). The design effect of less than one for the proportion of males makes sense since most households and neighborhood clusters are well balanced in the gender composition; clusters are heterogeneous, and the intraclass correlation is negative. The large design effect for the proportion of blacks reflects the current distribution of black population in the United States; clusters are homogeneous with respect to racial composition and the ICC should be highly positive. Similarly, the large design effect for the poverty index and education are highly associated with the race variable in the U.S. population.

Table 6.2 presents the results of the multiple regression for the body mass index on the selected variables under the three options of analysis. The first and second analyses were performed by the RE-GRESS procedure in BASS, and the third analysis was done using the REGRESSION procedure in PC CARP.

The results of the first analysis indicate that age is positively related and the age square term is negatively related to the body mass index. This indicates that the age effect is curvilinear with a dampening trend for older ages, as one might expect. Education and the poverty index are negatively associated with the body mass index. Examining the regression coefficients for the binary variables, the body mass index for blacks is 1.09 points higher than for nonblacks; that is, blacks are slightly more obese than nonblacks. Similarly, it is higher for the married than for the nonmarried. The users of vitamin supplements, who may be more concerned about their health, have a lower body mass index than the nonusers. The body mass index for smokers is 1.34 points lower than for nonsmokers. Finally, the coefficient for gender is relatively small but positive. The t-statistic indicates that the gender difference is statistically insignificant, but gender is retained in the model because its effect might change when the overrepresentation of the elderly is corrected. Such a change is anticipated in light of the diminishing age effect for old ages. The R-square value indicates that 10 percent of variation in the body mass index can be accounted for by these independent variables. For sim-

TABLE 6.2

Summary of Multiple Regression Models for Body Mass Index on Selected Variables for Adults 18-74 Years from NHANES II Under Three Different Analytic Options (n = 12,486)

Analytic Option	Variable	Regression Coefficient	Standard Error	Design Effect*	t-Statistic
1. Unweighted, ignoring the data structure:					
	Intercept	19.108	0.385	—	49.59
	Age in years	0.340	0.0178	—	19.14
	Age squared (/100)	−0.317	0.0192	—	−16.52
	Race (black)	1.091	0.137	—	7.97
	Gender (male)	0.016	0.086	—	0.19
	Marital status (married)	0.234	0.098	—	2.40
	Poverty index	−0.130	0.032	—	−4.07
	Education (yrs. of schooling)	−0.072	0.014	—	−5.22
	Vitamin supplement (yes)	−0.896	0.089	—	−10.04
	Smoking now (yes)	−1.344	0.091	—	−14.76
	(R-square = 0.102)				
2. Weighted, ignoring the data structure:					
	Intercept	19.095	0.371	—	51.45
	Age in years	0.336	0.0174	—	19.26
	Age squared (/100)	−0.314	0.0195	—	−16.06
	Race (black)	1.201	0.139	—	8.63
	Gender (male)	0.454	0.084	—	5.41
	Marital status (married)	0.298	0.097	—	3.07
	Poverty index	−0.132	0.031	—	−4.24
	Education (yrs. of schooling)	−0.098	0.014	—	−6.99
	Vitamin supplement (yes)	−0.805	0.087	—	−9.20
	Smoking now (yes)	−1.089	0.087	—	−12.46
	(R-square = 0.108)				
3. Weighted, considering the data structure:					
	Intercept	19.095	0.451	1.47	42.35
	Age in years	0.336	0.0179	1.06	18.77
	Age squared (/100)	−0.314	0.0190	0.95	−16.54
	Race (black)	0.201	0.205	2.18	5.85
	Gender (male)	0.454	0.112	1.78	4.05
	Marital status (married)	0.298	0.132	1.85	2.26
	Poverty index	−0.132	0.033	1.13	−3.95
	Education (yrs. of schooling)	−0.098	0.020	2.04	−5.01
	Vitamin supplement (yes)	−0.805	0.116	1.78	−6.94
	Smoking now (yes)	−1.089	0.078	0.80	−14.01
	(R-square = 0.108)				

*Square of the ratio of the standard error in (3) to the standard error in (2).

plicity, the interaction terms are not considered in this example, although their inclusion would undoubtedly have increased the R-square.

When the sample weights were used (the second option), the regression coefficients showed little change except for gender and smoking status. The coefficient for gender increased dramatically and became statistically significant. The gender effect was hidden in the unweighted analysis due to the overrepresentation of the elderly. The coefficient for smoking status decreased slightly in absolute value from 1.34 to 1.09, suggesting that the negative effect of smoking on the body mass index is more pronounced for the elderly than for younger adults.

When both the weight and the data structure were incorporated into the analysis, the standard errors of the coefficients and the t-statistics changed considerably. However there was no change in the estimated regression coefficients from those shown in the second analysis since the same formula is used in the two estimations. The design effects of the estimated variances of regression coefficients ranged from 0.80 for the smoking status to 2.18 for race. Again we see that a complex survey design may result in a larger variance for some variables than an SRS, but not necessarily for all the variables. Comparing the design effects in Tables 6.1 and 6.2, one notices the somewhat smaller design effects for regression coefficients than for means and proportions. In this particular example, the general analytic conclusions that were drawn in the preliminary analysis were also true in the final analysis, although the standard errors for regression coefficients were increased for all but one variable.

7. CONDUCTING CONTINGENCY TABLE ANALYSIS

Two methods for contingency table analysis introduced into social science research in recent years are the log-linear model (Goodman, 1970, 1971) and the weighted least squares (WLS) method (Grizzle et al., 1969). A nontechnical introduction to these methods for social scientists was given by Swafford (1980), and a detailed discussion for nonstatisticians was provided by Knoke and Burke (1980) for the log-linear model and by Forthofer and Lehnen (1981) for the WLS approach. The application of these two methods to the analysis of complex sample survey data is presented in this chapter. The WLS method is presented first and used to analyze data from a complex sample survey. This presentation is followed by a discussion of the log-linear model and an illustration of its use with the same data used in the WLS analysis.

The Weighted Least Squares Method for Complex Survey

The WLS method for categorical data is similar to regression and ANOVA in concept. The goal is to discover which predictor (independent) variables are related to the response (dependent) variable, and to describe the relation. This description is accomplished through the use of the general linear model with the parameters (coefficients) in the model describing the relation between the response and predictor variables. However, differences exist between the categorical data and regression situations that affect the estimation of the parameters. Two major differences are: (1) the dependent variable in the contingency table analysis is the cell proportion or some function of it, instead of the observations for individuals; and (2) the variances of the cell proportions are often unequal, whereas the variances of the observations of the dependent variable are assumed to be equal in regression analysis.

Because of these differences, the ordinary least squares (OLS) estimation used in regression analysis is replaced by the WLS estimation of the model parameters. Since the proportions or the functions of them may be correlated, the weights now are the elements of the inverse of the variance-covariance matrix of the cell proportions or of the function of the proportions. If there is zero correlation between the proportions or the functions, then the weights are simply the reciprocals of the variances of the proportions or the functions of proportions. This weighting adjusts for the unequal variances and gives more weight to the cells with the smaller variances.

The function is created by a combination of linear, logarithmic, or exponential transformations of the cell proportions. The combination of these transformations allows for the creation of a wide variety of dependent variables, for example, the proportion itself, the logit of the proportion, measures of association, and mean scores. After selecting the function, the steps in a WLS analysis are as follows: (1) to estimate the parameters of the model and their standard errors; (2) to obtain a measure of the adequacy of the fit of the model; and (3) to test hypotheses about the parameters if the model provides a reasonable fit to the data. Hence the ideas of regression and ANOVA can be used with contingency tables through the use of the WLS method. The test statistics for the goodness of fit and for the hypotheses about the parameters of the model asymptotically follow a chi-square distribution if the hypotheses are true.[5] Our experience suggests that most of the unweighted cell frequencies should be greater than 25 for the method to be used with confidence.

The dispersion matrix of cell proportions has the variances along the diagonal and the covariances on the off diagonal. For example, the dispersion matrix for the proportions (p) from a table consisting of 4 cells is as follows:

$$\text{Var}(p) = \begin{bmatrix} \text{var}(p_1) & \text{cov}(p_1, p_2) & \text{cov}(p_1, p_3) & \text{cov}(p_1, p_4) \\ \text{cov}(p_1, p_2) & \text{var}(p_2) & \text{cov}(p_2, p_3) & \text{cov}(p_2, p_4) \\ \text{cov}(p_1, p_3) & \text{cov}(p_2, p_3) & \text{var}(p_3) & \text{cov}(p_3, p_4) \\ \text{cov}(p_1, p_4) & \text{cov}(p_2, p_4) & \text{cov}(p_3, p_4) & \text{var}(p_4) \end{bmatrix} \quad [7.1]$$

Since Var (p) is symmetric, in an $r \times r$ dispersion matrix there are only $r \times (r + 1)/2$ unique elements. In the SRS or stratified random sampling framework, there are formulas for the variances and covariances of the cell proportions based on the binomial or multinomial distributions. However, in the complex survey framework no comparable formulas exist for the general situation. Therefore, it is necessary to employ one of the methods of Chapter 4 to estimate the variances and covariances of the cell proportions. This extension of the WLS approach to complex survey data was introduced by Koch et al. (1975).

The dispersion matrix estimated by incorporating the weights and the data structure, along with the weighted proportions, is then entered into a program that performs the WLS analysis for categorical data. This two-step approach can be used to perform many different types of analyses. Two simple functions are illustrated in the following section.

The WLS Method: An Example from NHANES II

The same data from NHANES II utilized for the regression analysis in the previous chapter were used to examine the relation between taking a vitamin supplement and the person's gender and education. The rows of the table are formed by the combination of the two levels of gender and the three levels of education, and the columns are usage and nonusage of a vitamin supplement. Since each row is considered as a separate subgroup, the proportions of users and nonusers sum to one within each subgroup. Hence only six proportions need to be analyzed.

Table 7.1 presents the unweighted and weighted frequency tables for this analysis. The unweighted cell frequencies are large enough for an analysis by the WLS method. In addition, an examination of the unweighted cross tabulation of the data by gender and education for each PSU (not shown in the table) showed no cells with fewer than five observations and most with at least ten observations. Hence, the data provide a sufficient number of observations to support the estimation of variances and covariances. Additionally, there are 32 degrees of freedom available (64 PSU – 32 strata) for this design and, thus, the estimation of the 21 variances and covariances resulting from the six proportions is possible.

Since the relative weights are used, the totals of the unweighted and weighted frequencies are the same, but the cell frequencies differ because of the weights. The unweighted proportions of people taking a vitamin supplement are not extreme, ranging from 0.25 for males with education less than a high school graduate to 0.50 for females with some college education. The proportion using a vitamin supplement is larger for females than males and for the more educated than the less educated. The weighted proportions are similar to the unweighted proportions for the respective cells, indicating that the weights have a minimal effect on the estimated proportions.

The analysis is performed under two analytic options to show the effect of incorporating the weights and the data structure into the analysis. The first analysis concerns the unweighted proportions ignoring the design features, and the second analysis deals with the weighted proportions incorporating the data structure. The dispersion matrices of the proportions for these two analyses are shown in Table 7.2. The matrix for the unweighted analysis contains the binomial variances on the diagonal, and the covariances are all zero. The estimation of the dispersion matrix for second analysis is a separate step using a program for computing variances and covariances for a complex survey.

The 6 × 6 dispersion matrix for the second analysis was estimated using the REGRESSION procedure in PC CARP. The dependent variable is a binary variable that has the value of 1 if the person took a vi-

TABLE 7.1

The Use of Vitamin Supplement by Gender and Education for
Unweighted and Weighted Data from NHANES II (n = 12,486)

Gender	Education	*Unweighted* User	Nonuser	Propor.	*Weighted* User	Nonuser	Propor.
Female:							
	<H.S. graduate	869	1670	0.342	711	1359	0.343
	H.S. graduate	948	1291	0.423	1046	1377	0.432
	Some college	892	910	0.495	1029	1017	0.503
Male:							
	<H.S. graduate	579	1762	0.247	424	1440	0.228
	H.S. graduate	502	1163	0.302	514	1239	0.293
	Some college	747	1153	0.393	925	1405	0.397
	Total	4537	7949	0.363	4649	7837	0.372

TABLE 7.2

Estimated Dispersion Matrix for the Unweighted and Weighted
Proportions Taking a Vitamin Supplement by Gender and Education
($x\ 10^4$)

Gender	Education	*Females* <HS	HS	>HS	*Males* <HS	HS	>HS
	1. For the unweighted proportions with no design features:						
Female:	<H.S. graduate	0.887	0	0	0	0	0
	H.S. graduate	0	1.090	0	0	0	0
	Some college	0	0	1.387	0	0	0
Male:	<H.S. graduate	0	0	0	0.795	0	0
	H.S. graduate	0	0	0	0	1.265	0
	Some college	0	0	0	0	0	1.256
	2. For the weighted proportions with the design features:						
Female:	<H.S. graduate	2.199	0.421	0.111	0.584	0.506	−0.207
	H.S. graduate	0.421	2.258	0.062	0.071	0.196	0.666
	Some college	0.111	1.062	3.104	−0.021	0.224	0.622
Male:	<H.S. graduate	0.584	0.071	−0.021	1.428	0.130	−0.231
	H.S. graduate	0.506	0.196	0.224	0.130	1.553	−0.054
	Some college	−0.207	0.666	0.622	−0.231	−0.054	1.547

tamin supplement and 0 otherwise. The independent variables are 6 binary variables corresponding to the 6 levels of the combined gender by education variables. The first independent variable refers to the females who have not graduated from high school. It takes the value of 1 if the person considered is a female who has not graduated from high school and 0 otherwise. The other independent variables are similarly defined. The REGRESSION procedure in PC CARP allows the user to eliminate the constant term (intercept) from the regression equation. Excluding the constant means that the dependent variable (1 or 0) is a function solely of the gender and education cell to which the person belongs. This is the cell-mean model in the ANOVA framework. The estimated regression coefficients in this model are the proportion taking a vitamin supplement in each of the six cells. The dispersion matrix of the regression coefficients contains then the variances and covariances for the weighted cell proportions.

The differences between the first and second matrices should be noted. The estimated variances, the diagonal elements, in the second matrix are considerably larger than those in the first matrix. For example, the complex variance of the proportion using a vitamin supplement for females who did not graduate from high school is 2.199×10^{-4} in the second matrix. This is 2.5 times larger than the corresponding simple variance (0.887×10^{-4}) in the first matrix, a sizable design effect. The covariances in the second matrix are nonzero, reflecting the dependency between observations due to the complex design in NHANES II.

This completes the first step in the application of the WLS method to a contingency table analysis. The next step is to pass the cell proportions and their dispersion matrix to a program that performs the WLS analysis of contingency tables. Two models are considered for each analytic option: additive and multiplicative. In the additive model the proportion itself is the dependent variable, that is

$$\begin{pmatrix} \text{proportion} \\ \text{taking } vitamins \end{pmatrix} = [\text{constant}] + \begin{pmatrix} \text{gender} \\ \text{effect} \end{pmatrix} + \begin{pmatrix} \text{education} \\ \text{effect} \end{pmatrix}$$

The multiplicative model analyzes the logit of the weighted proportion taking a vitamin supplement. If p represents the proportion taking a supplement, the multiplicative model is

$$[\log\{p/(1-p)\}] = [\text{constant}] + \begin{pmatrix} \text{gender} \\ \text{effect} \end{pmatrix} + \begin{pmatrix} \text{education} \\ \text{effect} \end{pmatrix}$$

This is the natural logarithm of the odds that a person in a particular sex by education group is taking a vitamin supplement. The interpretation of the parameters is in terms of the log-odds of taking a vitamin supplement.

The use of the proportion as the dependent variable means that one is considering an additive relation among the variables, whereas the use of the logit says that one is considering the relation among the variables to be multiplicative. Other transformations of the proportions are possible as well, but we shall not consider them in this example. The choice of which function of the proportion to use depends on the investigator's perspective. As long as the proportion is not too extreme, the results of the analyses should be similar. However, there can be a difference in the results if many of the proportions are less than 0.25 or greater than 0.75. The multiplicative model is considered here to facilitate a comparison with the results of a log-linear model analysis to be presented in the next section.

The data required for the additive model analysis are in Tables 7.1 and 7.2, and the WLS analysis was performed using the CATMOD procedure in PC SAS. These data need to be transformed for the multiplicative model analysis. The transformation of the proportions in Table 7.1 into the log-odds is straightforward. Table 7.3 contains the unweighted and weighted odds and the log-odds of taking a vitamin supplement. The transformation of the dispersion matrices in Table 7.3 required a series of matrix manipulations.[6] These manipulations and the associated WLS analysis were performed using the matrix commands in MINITAB. The dispersion matrices for the unweighted and weighted log-odds are shown in Table 7.4.

Table 7.5 shows the results of both the additive and multiplicative analyses of these data when the data structure and weights are incorporated as well as when they are excluded. The parameter estimates (the constant, gender effects and education effects) and their estimated standard errors are shown, as well as the corresponding test statistics. The interpretation of the additive results is straightforward. First, the goodness-of-fit statistic suggests that the main effects model fits the data; in this simple situation, the two degrees of freedom associated with the goodness of fit of the model can also be interpreted as the two degrees of freedom associated with the gender by education interaction. Hence, there is no interaction of gender and education in relation to the proportion using a vitamin supplement. Both the gender and education variables are highly significant regardless of

TABLE 7.3

The Unweighted and Weighted Odds and Log-Odds of Taking a
Vitamin Supplement for Persons Age 18-74 from NHANES II
by Gender and Education Groups

		Unweighted		Weighted	
Gender	Education	Odds $p/(1-p)$	Log-Odds $\ln[p/(1-p)]$	Odds $p/(1-p)$	Log-Odds $\ln[p/1-p)]$
Female:	<H.S. graduate	0.520	−0.653	0.522	−0.650
	H.S. graduate	0.734	−0.309	0.761	−0.274
	Some college	0.980	−0.020	1.012	−0.012
Male:	<H.S. graduate	0.329	−1.113	0.295	−1.220
	H.S. graduate	0.432	−0.840	0.414	−0.881
	Some college	0.648	−0.434	0.658	−0.418
	Total	0.571	−0.560	0.592	−0.524

TABLE 7.4

Estimated Dispersion Matrix for the Unweighted and Weighted
Log-Odds of Taking a Vitamin Supplement by Gender and Education
$(x\ 10^3)$

		Females			Males		
Gender	Education	<HS	HS	>HS	<HS	HS	>HS
1. For the unweighted proportions with no design features:							
Female:	<H.S. graduate	1.750	0	0	0	0	0
	H.S. graduate	0	1.829	0	0	0	0
	Some college	0	0	2.220	0	0	0
Male:	<H.S. graduate	0	0	0	2.295	0	0
	H.S. graduate	0	0	0	0	2.852	0
	Some college	0	0	0	0	0	2.206
2. For the weighted proportions with the design features:							
Female:	<H.S. graduate	4.325	0.761	0.197	1.472	1.083	−0.383
	H.S. graduate	0.761	3.752	1.732	0.164	0.386	1.134
	Some college	0.197	1.732	4.967	−0.048	0.432	1.039
Male:	<H.S. graduate	0.472	0.164	−0.048	4.613	0.357	−0.548
	H.S. graduate	1.083	0.386	0.432	0.357	3.616	−0.109
	Some college	−0.383	1.134	1.039	−0.548	−0.109	2.699

TABLE 7.5

Weighted and Unweighted Parameter Estimates and Test Statistics for Additive and Multiplicative Models of Vitamin Use

Statistics		*Unweighted Analysis*		*Weighted Analysis**	
ADDITIVE MODEL					
Parameter:		Estimate	Std. Error	Estimate	Std. Error
Constant		0.367	0.0043	0.366	0.0074
Female Effect		0.053	0.0042	0.060	0.0051
< HS Effect		−0.077	0.0064	−0.079	0.0089
HS Effect		0.004	0.0062	−0.004	0.0063
Test statistics:	df	Chi-square	p-value	Chi-square	p-value
Gender	1	154.07	<0.0001	136.72	<0.0001
Education	2	207.33	<0.0001	101.77	<0.0001
Goodness of fit	2	1.85	0.40	1.71	0.43
MULTIPLICATIVE MODEL					
Parameter:		Estimate	Std. Error	Estimate	Std. Error
Constant		−0.559	0.0190	−0.564	0.0327
Female Effect		0.234	0.0191	0.306	0.0224
< HS Effect		−0.324	0.0262	−0.357	0.0425
HS Effect		−0.008	0.0271	−0.009	0.0282
Test statistics:	df	Chi-square	p-value	Chi-square	p-value
Gender	1	149.76	<0.0001	140.39	<0.0001
Education	2	204.76	<0.0001	95.90	<0.0001
Goodness of fit	2	1.53	0.47	3.05	0.22

*Incorporating the data structure.

whether the weights and the data structure are considered. However, the estimated standard errors of the coefficients are considerably larger for the weighted data than for the unweighted data.

Since effect coding was used, the effects of all categories of a factor should sum to zero. The male effect (not shown in the table) is then equal to minus the female effect, and, similarly, the effect of more than a high school education is minus the sum of the effects of less than a high school education and a high school education. Hence, females and those with greater than a high school education have the higher usage of vitamins. Females have a proportion of vitamin usage approximately 11 to 12 percent (two times the female parameter estimate) higher than males, and those with greater than a high school education have a proportion of vitamin usage about 15 to 16 percent greater than those with less than a high school education.

The main effect multiplicative model also fits the data, and again both main effects are highly significant. The interpretation of the parameters is now in terms of the log-odds; if we take the exponential of the parameter estimates, then the interpretation is in terms of the odds, which may be easier to understand. In the weighted analysis, which incorporates the data structure, the exponential of the constant (exp $\{-0.564\}$) is 0.569. This is an approximation to the overall ratio of the proportion of vitamin usage to the proportion of non-usage. The exponential of the estimate of the female effect is 1.357 (exp $\{0.306\}$). This means that the estimate of the odds of vitamin usage for females is 1.357 times the overall value of 0.569; hence, the estimate of the odds for females is 0.772. The male effect is exp $\{-0.306\} = 0.736$, and the estimate of the odds for males is then $0.569 \times 0.736 = 0.419$. The effect of education can be considered in the same fashion.

There is very little change for the goodness-of-fit test statistics or for the gender variable when going from the unweighted to the weighted analysis which incorporated the data structure. However, the test statistic for the education variable was reduced by approximately 50 percent, although it remained highly significant. There is little difference between the additive and multiplicative results, and this was expected since the values of the proportions ranged from 0.23 to 0.50.

Using this two-step procedure, practically the full range of analyses available under the WLS approach to contingency table analysis can be used with complex survey data. Additional examples of the use of this approach with complex survey data are given by Landis et al. (1982) and by Lee et al. (1986b).

Log-Linear Models for Complex Survey Data

In addition to the references cited earlier, the books by Haberman (1974, 1978), Fienberg (1977), and Bishop et al. (1975) present the maximum likelihood (ML) approach to log-linear models and additional examples of the application of the approach to contingency table analysis. In the log-linear model, the natural logarithm of the cell proportion is expressed as a linear combination of the effects of the variables that make up the table. This relation is also a multiplicative one among the variables that form the table. The equation for this for a table with three variables is

$$\log(p_{ijk}) = \mu + \lambda_i^I + \lambda_j^J + \lambda_k^K + \lambda_{ij}^{IJ} + \lambda_{ik}^{IK} + \lambda_{jk}^{JK} \qquad [7.2]$$

We assume that

$$\sum \lambda_i^I = \sum \lambda_j^J = \sum \lambda_k^K = 0;$$

$$\sum_i \lambda_{ij}^{IJ} = \sum_i \lambda_{ik}^{IK} = \sum_j \lambda_{jk}^{JK} = \sum_j \lambda_{ij}^{IJ} = \sum_k \lambda_{ik}^{IK} = \sum_k \lambda_{jk}^{JK} = 0.$$

These are the usual assumptions for effect coding in the ANOVA. This model states that the natural logarithm of the probability of any cell can be expressed as the sum of a constant term, the main effects of variables I, J, and K and their two-way interactions. This model does not include a three-way interaction term, but it could be added since terms are added to or deleted from the model as needed to provide a parsimonious model that gives an adequate fit to the data. Maximum likelihood estimation is used to obtain estimates of the parameters in the model. The goodness of fit of the model is determined by substituting the maximum likelihood estimates of the cell probabilities in the formula for the Pearson chi-square statistic,

$$X^2 = \sum (O_i - E_i)^2 / E_i$$

or in the likelihood ratio chi-square statistic,

$$G^2 = \sum O_i * \ln(O_i / E_i) \qquad [7.3]$$

where O_i is the observed i-th cell proportion and E_i is the ML estimate of this cell proportion. The importance of a term in the model is determined by comparing two models, one that is considered as a base model, and another model that includes the term of interest in addition to all the other terms in the base model. The difference in the likelihood ratio chi-square goodness-of-fit statistics is itself distributed as a chi-square statistic and is the test statistic for determining if the effect of the term is zero. This test of whether a term's effect is zero depends on the base model.

Many applications of the ML method focus on the logit of one of the variables in the model. Using the above notation, let I represent the usage or nonusage of vitamin supplements, J represent the education variable, and K be the gender variable. One model using the logit of the usage of a vitamin supplement based on the above equation is

$$\log\left(p_{1jk}/p_{2jk}\right) = \log\left(p_{1jk}\right) - \log\left(p_{2jk}\right)$$

$$= \mu + \lambda_1^I + \lambda_j^J + \lambda_k^K + \lambda_{1j}^{IJ} + \lambda_{1k}^{IK} + \lambda_{jk}^{JK}$$

$$- \left(\mu + \lambda_2^I + \lambda_j^J + \lambda_k^K + \lambda_{2j}^{IJ} + \lambda_{2k}^{IK} + \lambda_{jk}^{JK} \right)$$

$$= \left(\lambda_1^I - \lambda_2^I\right) + \left(\lambda_{1j}^{IJ} - \lambda_{2j}^{IJ}\right) + \left(\lambda_{1k}^{IK} - \lambda_{2k}^{IK}\right). \qquad [7.4]$$

Using the assumptions about the parameters given above, and since there are only two levels for variable I, we have

$$\log\left(p_{1jk}/p_{2jk}\right) = 2\left(\lambda_1^I + \lambda_{1j}^{IJ} + \lambda_{1k}^{IK}\right) \qquad [7.5]$$

This is the same equation examined in the WLS section when the multiplicative function was selected as the dependent variable in the analysis. This model is interpreted as saying that the logit of taking a vitamin supplement can be expressed as the sum of a constant and the main effects of the education and gender variables. Note that the main effect of an independent variable on the dependent variable is really an interaction of the independent variable with the dependent variable. Hence the main effect of education on the logit is simply twice the effect of the interaction of education and the vitamin supplement variable.

Fay (1985) has extended these ideas to the complex sample survey. He uses the replication idea discussed in Chapter 4 to obtain estimates of the standard error of the model parameters and the test statistic for testing the goodness of fit of the model. The replication idea is implemented through either the jackknife, the stratified jackknife, or pseudo half-sample replication. The choice of which of these three approaches to use depends on the sample design, and Fay (1983) provides guidance in making this choice. He recommends forming from 20 to 50 replicates of the weighted sample data, and, for each of these replicates, the log-linear or logit model under consideration is fitted. The test statistic for the fit of the model, as well as the parameter estimates, is retained for each replicate and used in the estimation of the complex sample survey adjusted goodness-of-fit statistics and standard errors of the parameters.

There are two goodness-of-fit statistics, one, X_J, based on the Pearson chi-square and the other, G_J, based on the likelihood ratio statistic. The distribution function is not known for either of these statistics, but Fay (1983) has performed extensive simulations and provided a table that gives the critical values for significance levels ranging from 0.1 to 0.001 for a limited number of degrees of freedom. The test statistics X_J and G_J have the same distribution, and it generally approaches the normal distribution as the degrees of freedom increase.

The program CPLX (Fay, 1983) implements the ML log-linear model approach to categorical data collected via a complex sample survey. It uses the iterative proportional fitting estimation routine and is, therefore, limited to hierarchical models. There are two main inputs to CPLX. The first set of inputs is very similar to the input to ECTA (Haberman, 1978, 1979) and sets up the structure of the data and describes the models that are to be analyzed. The second set of inputs contains the data to be analyzed, including replicate codes, replicates, and the weights.

Log-Linear (Logit) Models: An Example from NHANES II

We shall consider the same problem that was used in the WLS section to demonstrate the use of logit models with complex survey data. The unweighted ML analysis in this section was performed using the ML option in CATMOD in PC SAS. The analysis incorporating the weight and the data structure was performed by the PC version of CPLX. Since the NHANES II design is being treated as a selection of two PSUs per pseudo-stratum, the stratified jackknife option in CPLX was chosen for the analysis. This choice requires that the PSUs are numbered consecutively and the number of PSUs in each stratum be specified. The input data need to be sorted by PSU.

To be able to compare the results with the previous analysis by the WLS approach, we will treat the logit of usage of a vitamin supplement as the dependent variable. The models are specified to test the hypotheses of no education by gender interaction, no education effect given a main effects model, and no gender effect given a main effects model. Unlike the WLS approach, which required the fitting of only one model to find these three statistics, it is necessary to fit four models to obtain these statistics with the ML approach.

The models shown below take advantage of the hierarchical idea in their expression. Hierarchical means that if a higher order term is specified as being in the model, then all lower order relatives of that term are also included in the model. Using V for the use of vitamin supplement, E for education, and G for gender, the models fitted are

1. (VEG),
2. (VE, VG, EG),
3. (VG, EG),
4. (VE, EG).

The first model includes the three-way interaction term of VEG and all its lower order relatives: VE, VG, EG, V, E, and G. From the logit perspective, there is no interest in the terms that do not involve V, the dependent variable. However, the EG term and its lower order relatives must be included to indicate that these margins are also fixed, although they are being viewed as fixed in advance. This model says that the logit is expressed as a constant (V), the main effects of education (VE) and gender (VG) and the interaction of education and gender (VEG).

The second model includes the required EG term and its lower order relatives as well as the constant term (V), the main effects of education (VE) and gender (VG) on the logit, but no interaction of education and gender (VEG) on the logit. Thus the difference in the goodness-of-fit statistics between models 2 and 1 tests the hypothesis of no education by gender interaction on the logit. The third and fourth models are defined similarly, and the difference between the goodness-of-fit statistics for models 3 and 2 tests the hypothesis of no education effect on the logit, and the difference in the goodness-of-fit statistics for models 4 and 2 tests the hypothesis of no gender effect.

TABLE 7.6

Weighted and Unweighted Parameter Estimates and Test Statistics for
the Logit (Multiplicative) Model of Vitamin Use

Statistics		Unweighted Analysis		Weighted Anaalysis*	
		Estimate	Std. Error	Estimate	Std. Error
Parameter:					
Constant		−0.559	0.019	−0.572	0.034
Female		0.234	0.019	0.268	0.022
< HS Effect		−0.332	0.027	−0.368	0.038
HS Effect		0.008	0.027	0.006	0.030
Test statistics:	df	Likelihood Ratio X^2	p-value	G_S	Design effect**	p-value
Gender	1	150.01	<0.0001	14.65	(1.50)	<0.0001
Education	2	204.41	<0.0001	11.83	(2.58)	<0.0001
Goodness-of-fit	2	1.53	0.46	0.50	(1.38)	0.21

*Incorporating the design features.
**"Effective average design effect."

This information, that is, the number of variables and their levels as
well as what models to consider, is an important part of the first set of
inputs to CPLX.

The results of this analysis and the unweighted ML analysis are
shown in Table 7.6. The unweighted ML results from CATMOD are
very similar to the unweighted WLS results (multiplicative model)
shown in Table 7.5, and this is to be expected since the sample size
is large. Additionally, the ML results based on the weights and the
data structure from CPLX agree quite well with the corresponding
WLS results. To obtain this agreement, we had to remember to mul-
tiply the CPLX parameter estimates and estimates of standard error
by two as was pointed out in equation 7.5 and the discussion following it. The differences between the unweighted and weighted analyses
are also consistent with those in the WLS analysis. In addition to G_J,
CPLX provides "effective average design effect" to indicate the combined effects of the sample design features for all categories of the
variable. As in the WLS analysis, the design effect is considerable for
education.

WLS Method and Log-Linear Models: Which to Use?

WLS and ML are both general approaches to the analysis of contingency tables and give similar results in most cases,[7] as shown in the previous section. The key difference that we see between the methods are in their range of application. One consideration is in terms of the size of the table that the procedure can handle. The ML approach can be applied to much larger contingency tables than can the WLS approach. The sample size requirements are less stringent for the ML approach because, for example, in the logit case the sample size requirements focus only on the margin totals, whereas the WLS approach focuses on individual cell counts. The WLS approach probably should not be used for tables with more than six variables, and if the variables have several levels, perhaps only four or five variables can be used. The ML method can be used with tables having a larger number of cells.

A second consideration is the type of problem that can be addressed by the procedure. Here the WLS approach has the advantage because it is not limited to the log-linear hierarchical framework. The WLS approach allows the user to choose the scale for the analysis, for example, to analyze the proportion itself or some other function of the dependent variable(s) instead of the logit.

In analyzing categorical data from a complex survey, the WLS approach has the advantage because it can be interfaced with any program that calculates variances and covariances for a complex survey. All three methods (BRR, JRR, and the Taylor series approximation) can be used. The log-linear model approach is limited to a replication-based method of variance calculation adapted to the maximum likelihood estimation.

8. CONCLUDING REMARKS

In this book we have discussed the problematic aspects of survey data analysis and methods for dealing with the difficulties caused by the use of complex sample designs. The focus has been on the understanding of the problem and the logic of the methods, rather than providing a technical manual. We have also presented a practical guide for preparing for an analysis of complex survey data and demonstrated the use of some of the software available for performing regression and contingency table analyses.

Though the material presented on these issues has been addressed mainly to the survey data analyst, we hope that this introduction also stimulates the survey designers and data preparers to pay more attention to the needs of the users of survey data. As more analytic uses are made of the data initially collected for enumerative purposes, the survey designers must consider including certain design features that allow more appropriate analysis to be performed, as well as ease the users' burden. The data preparers should develop the weights appropriate to the sample design and include codes for strata and PSUs in the data files.

Finally, we must point out that we have been taking the position of design-based statistical inference. The opposing view is that of model-based inference. There is an ongoing debate between these two points of view (Royall, 1970; Smith, 1976, 1983; Sarnadal, 1978; Hansen et al., 1983). Briefly, the model-based inference assumes that a sample is a convenience set of observations from a conceptual super-population. The population parameters under the specified model are of primary interest, and the sample selection scheme is considered secondary to the inference. Consequently, the role of the sample design is de-emphasized here, and statistical estimation uses the prediction approach under the specified model. Naturally, estimates are subject to bias if the model is misspecified, and the bias can be substantial even in large samples. The design-based inference requires taking into account the sample design, and it is the traditional approach. The finite population is of primary interest, and the analysis aims at finding estimates that are design-unbiased in repeated sampling.

We believe that the sample design does matter when inference is made from sample data, especially in the description of social phenomena, in comparison to more predictable physical phenomena. At the same time, the appropriateness of a model needs to be assessed in any data analysis. Any inference using both the design and model is likely to be more successful than that using either one alone.

NOTES

1. Holt and Smith (1979) characterized poststratification as a robust technique for estimation. Based on the conditional distribution, they showed that the self-weighted sample mean is in general biased, contrary to the usual position, and poststratification offers protection against extreme sample configurations. They suggested that poststratification should be more strongly considered for use in sample surveys than appears to be the case at present. By the same token, it could also provide protection against any anomalies introduced by nonresponse and other problems in sample selection.

2. The method of ratio estimation is used not only in estimating the population ratio of two variables (e.g., the ratio of the weight of fruits and the amount of juice produced) but also in obtaining a more accurate estimate of a variable (e.g., current income, y) by forming a ratio to another closely related variable (e.g., previous income at the time of the last census, x). The sample ratio (y/x or change in income) is then applied to the previous census income to obtain the current estimate of income, which is more accurate than that estimated without using the subsidiary variable. For details see Cochran (1977, Chapter 6).

3. The PC version of CPLX was provided by Dr. Fay of the U.S. Bureau of the Census. Although some new features are added, it is similar to the mainframe version.

4. One way of directly accounting for this correlation would be to include a random term in the model for each household or classroom. This would remove this source of variation in the data from the random error component in the model. In so doing, the estimates of the parameters of interest should not be greatly affected, but their variance estimates would be changed because the estimate of the error variance would be very different compared to the error variance from the model without these random terms. However, this direct way of accounting for the correlation is not feasible because the size of the model quickly becomes too large, and there would be insufficient degrees of freedom for the estimation of the dispersion matrix of the parameter estimates.

5. A Wald statistic with one degree of freedom is basically the square of a normal variable with a mean of zero divided by its standard deviation. For hypotheses involving more than one degree of freedom, the Wald statistic is the matrix extension of the square of the normal variable.

6. The transformation of the dispersion matrix for the log-odds involves several steps of matrix manipulation. For details see Forthofer and Lehnen (1981).

7. Both are BAN (best asymptotic normal) methods, and, hence, in the asymptotic case, there is little difference between the methods. There may be differences between the methods in the small sample case, but these have yet to be documented clearly. It is relatively easy to incorporate the ordinality of the independent and dependent variables into the analysis with the WLS approach. The ML approach is limited in this regard, although a multi-step approach can be used to deal with the ordinality. GLIM (Baker and Nelder, 1978) and MULTIQUAL (Bock and Yates, 1973) are two other programs that employ the ML method and take ordinality into account for the SRS case. See Swafford (1980) for an additional discussion of the merits of the WLS and the ML log-linear model approach.

REFERENCES

ANDREWS, F. F., J. N. MORGAN, and J. A. SONQUIST (1973) Multiple Classification Analysis (2nd ed.). Ann Arbor: Institute for Social Research, University of Michigan.

BAKER, R. J. and J. A. NELDER (1978) The GLIM System Release 3: Generalized Linear Interactive Modelling Manual. Oxford: Numerical Algorithms Group.

BASS Institute (1988) BASS™ Reference Manual. Chapel Hill, NC: Bass Institute Press.

BEAN, J. A. (1975) Distribution and Properties of Variance Estimators for Complex Multistage Probability Samples: An Empirical Distribution. Vital and Health Statistics, Series 2, No. 65, National Center for Health Statistics.

BISHOP, Y. M. M., S. E. FIENBERG, and P. W. HOLLAND (1975) Discrete Multivariate Analysis. Cambridge: MIT Press.

BOCK, R. D. and G. YATES (1973) "MULTIQUAL, log-linear analysis of nominal and ordinal qualitative data by the method of maximum likelihood: A FORTRAN program." Chicago: National Educational Resources.

CHAO, M. T. and S. H. LO (1985) "A bootstrap method for finite population." Sankhya 47 (Series A): 399-405.

COCHRAN, W. G. (1977) Sampling Techniques (3rd ed.). New York: John Wiley.

COHEN, S. B., J. A. XANTHOPOULOS, and G. K. JONES (1988) "An evaluation of statistical software procedures appropriate for regression analysis of complex survey data." Journal of Official Statistics 4(1):17-34.

DAVIS, J. A. and T. W. SMITH (1985) General Social Survey, 1972-1985: Cumulative Codebook, NORC Edition. National Opinion Research Center, University of Chicago and the Roper Center, University of Connecticut.

DEMING, W. E. (1960) Sample Design in Business Research. New York: John Wiley.

DuMOUCHEL, W. H. and G. J. DUNCAN (1983) "Using sample survey weights in multiple regression analysis of stratified samples." Journal of the American Statistical Association 78:535-543.

DURBIN, J. (1959) "A note on the application of Quenouille's method of bias reduction to the estimation of ratios." Biometrika 46: 477-480.

EFRON, B. (1979) "Bootstrap methods: Another look at the jackknife." Annals of Statistics 7:1-26.

FAY, R. E. (1983) CPLX—Contingency Table Analysis for Complex Sample Designs: Program Documentation. U.S. Bureau of the Census.

FAY, R. E. (1985) "A jackknife chi-square test for complex samples." Journal of the American Statistical Association 80:148-157.

FIENBERG, S. E. (1977) The Analysis of Cross-Classified Categorical Data. Cambridge: MIT Press.

FLYER, P. and L. MOHADJER (1988) The WESVAR Procedure. Rockville, MD: Westat.

FORTHOFER, R. N. and R. G. LEHNEN (1981) Public Program Analysis: A Categorical Data Approach. Belmont, CA: Lifetime Learning Publications.

75

76

FRANKEL, M. R. (1971) Inference from Survey Samples. Ann Arbor: Institute of Social Research, University of Michigan.

FULLER, W. A. (1975) "Regression analysis for sample surveys." Sankhya, 37 (Series C):117-132.

FULLER, W. A., W. KENNEDY, D. SCHNELL, G. SULLIVAN, and H. J. PARK (1986) PC CARP. Ames: Statistical Laboratory, Iowa State University.

GOODMAN, L. A. (1970) "The multivariate analysis of qualitative data: Interactions among multiple classifications." Journal of the American Statistical Association 65:226-256.

GOODMAN, L. A. (1971) "The analysis of multidimensional contingency tables: Stepwise procedures and direct estimation methods for building models for multiple classifications." Technometrics 13:33-61.

GOODMAN, L. A. (1972a) "A general model for the analysis of surveys." American Journal of Sociology 77:1035-1086.

GOODMAN, L. A. (1972b) "A modified multiple regression approach to the analysis of dichotomous variables." American Sociological Review 37:28-45.

GOODMAN, L. A. (1979) "A brief guide to the causal analysis of data from surveys." American Journal of Sociology 84:1078-1095.

GOODMAN, R. and L. KISH (1950) "Controlled selection: A technique in probability sampling." Journal of the American Statistical Association 45(251):350-373.

GRIZZLE, J. E., C. F. STARMER, and G. G. KOCH (1969) "Analysis of categorical data by linear models." Biometrics 25:489-504.

GURNEY, M. and R. S. JEWETT (1975) "Constructing orthogonal replications for variance estimation." Journal of the American Statistical Association 70:819-821.

HABERMAN, S. J. (1974) The Analysis of Frequency Data. Chicago: University of Chicago Press.

HABERMAN, S. J. (1978, 1979) The Analysis of Qualitative Data, Vols. 1-2. New York: Academic Press.

HANSEN, M. H., W. G. MADOW, and B. J. TEPPING (1983) "An evaluation of model-dependent and probability-sampling inferences in sample surveys." Journal of the American Statistical Association 78:776-807.

HIDIROGLOU, M. A., W. A. FULLER, and R. D. HICKMAN (1980) SUPER CARP. Ames: Survey Section, Statistical Laboratory, Iowa State University.

HOLT, D. and T. M. F. SMITH (1979) "Post stratification." Journal of the Royal Statistical Society 142 (Series A): 33-46.

HOLT, D., T. M. F. SMITH, and P. D. WINTER (1980) "Regression analysis of data from complex surveys." Journal of the Royal Statistical Society 143 (Series A): 474-487.

HOLT, M. M. (1977) SURREGR: Standard Errors of Regression Coefficients from Sample Survey Data. Research Triangle Park, NC: Research Triangle Institute. (Revised by B. V. Shah in 1982).

KALTON, G. (1983) Introduction to Survey Sampling. Sage University Papers 35: Quantitative Applications in the Social Sciences.

KENDALL, P. A. and P. F. LAZARSFELD (1950) "Problems of survey analysis," in R. K. Merton and P. F. Lazarsfeld (eds.) Continuities in Social Research: Studies in the Scope and Method of "The American Soldier." New York: Free Press.

KIECOLT, K. J. and L. E. NATHAN (1985) Secondary Analysis of Survey Data. Sage University Papers 53: Quantitative Applications in the Social Sciences.

KISH, L. (1949) "A procedure for objective respondent selection within the household." Journal of the American Statistical Association 44:380-387.

KISH, L. (1965) Survey Sampling. New York: John Wiley.

KISH, L. and M. R. FRANKEL (1974) "Inferences from complex samples." Journal of the Royal Statistical Society 36 (Series B): 1-37.

KNOKE, D. and P. J. BURKE (1980) Log-Linear Models. Beverly Hills, CA: Sage.

KOCH, G. G., D. H. FREEMAN, and J. L. FREEMAN (1975) "Strategies in the multivariate analysis of data from complex surveys." International Statistical Review 43:59-78.

KONIJN, H. (1962) "Regression analysis in sample surveys." Journal of the American Statistical Association 57:590-605.

KREWSKI, D. and J. N. K. RAO (1981) "Inference from stratified samples: Properties of the linearization, jackknife and balanced repeated replication methods." Annals of Statistics 9:1010-1019.

LANDIS, J. R., J. M. LEPKOWSKI, S. A. EKLUND, and S. A. STEHOUWER (1982) A Statistical Methodology for Analyzing Data from a Complex Sample Survey: The First National Health and Nutrition Examination Survey. Vital and Health Statistics Series 2, No. 92 National Center for Health Statistics.

LEE, E. S., R. N. FORTHOFER, C. E. HOLZER, and C. A. TAUBE (1986a) "Complex survey data analysis: Estimation of standard errors using pseudostrata." Journal of Economic and Social Measurement 14:135-144.

LEE, E. S., R. N. FORTHOFER, and R. J. LORIMOR (1986b) "Analysis of complex sample survey data: Problems and strategies." Sociological Methods and Research 15:69-100.

LEE, K. H. (1972) "The use of partially balanced designs for the half-sample replication method of variance estimation." Journal of the American Statistical Association 67:324-334.

LEMESHOW, S. and P. S. LEVY (1979) "Estimating the variance of ratio estimates in complex surveys with two primary sampling units per stratum: A comparison of balanced replication and jackknife techniques." Journal of Statistical Computing and Simulation 8:191-205.

LEVY, P. S. and S. LEMESHOW (1980) Sampling for Health Professionals. Belmont, CA: Lifetime Learning.

McCARTHY, P. J. (1986) Replication: An Approach to the Analysis of Data from Complex Surveys. Vital and Health Stat. Rep., Series 2, No. 14. National Center for Health Statistics.

McDOWELL, A., A. ENGEL, J. T. MASSEY, and K. MAURER (1981) Plan and Operation of the Second National Health and Nutrition Examination Survey, 1976-80. Vital and Health Stat. Rep., Series 1, No. 15. National Center for Health Statistics.

NATHAN, G. and D. HOLT (1980) "The effect of survey design on regression analysis." Journal of the Royal Statistical Society 42 (Series B): 377-386.

PFEFFERMANN, D. and G. NATHAN (1981) "Regression analysis of data from a cluster sample." Journal of the American Statistical Association 76:681-689.

PLACKETT, R. L. and P. J. BURMAN (1946) "The design of optimum multifactorial experiments." Biometrika 33: 305-325.

QUENOUILLE, M. H. (1949) "Approximate tests of correlation in time series." Journal of the Royal Statistical Society 11 (Series B): 68-84.

ROYALL, R. M. (1970) "On finite population sampling theory under certain linear regression models." Biometrika 57:377-387.

RYAN, T., B. JOINER, and B. RYAN (1975) MINITAB II, Reference Manual. The Pennsylvania State University.

SARNADAL, C. E. (1978) "Design-based and model-based inference in survey sampling." Scandinavian Journal of Statistics 5:25-52.

SAS INSTITUTE (1985) SAS Language Guide for Personal Computers, Version 6 Edition. Cary, NC: SAS Institute.

SHAH, B. V. (1980) SESUDAAN: Standard Air Program for Computing Standardized Rates from Sample Survey Data. Report from Research at Triangle Institute. Triangle Park, North Carolina.

SHAH, B. V., M. H. HOLT, and R. E. FOLSOM (1977) "Inference about regression models from sample survey data." Bulletin of the International Statistical Institute 47:43-57.

SMITH, T. M. F. (1976) "The foundations of survey sampling: A review." Journal of the Royal Statistical Society 139 (Series A): 183-204.

SMITH, T. M. F. (1983) "On the validity of inferences on non-random samples." Journal of the Royal Statistical Society 146 (Series A): 394-403.

STANEK, E. J. and S. LEMESHOW (1977) "The behavior of balanced half-sample variance estimates for linear and combined ratio estimates when strata are paired to form pseudo strata." American Statistical Association Proceedings: Social Statistics Section: 837-842.

STEPHAN, F. F. (1948) "History of the uses of modern sampling procedures." Journal of the American Statistical Association 43:12-39.

SUDMAN, S. (1976) Applied Sampling. New York: Academic Press.

SWAFFORD, M. (1980) "Three parametric techniques for contingency table analysis: non-technical commentary." American Sociological Review 45:604-690.

TEPPING, B. J. (1968) "Variance estimation in complex surveys." American Statistical Association Proceedings of Social Statistics Section: 11-18.

TUKEY, J. W. (1958) "Bias and confidence in not quite large samples." Annals of Mathematical Statistics 29:614.

TUKEY, J. W. (1986) "Sunset salvo." American Statistician 40:72-76.

WOLTER, K. M. (1985) Introduction to Variance Estimation. New York: Springer-Verlag.

WOODRUFF, R. S. (1971) "A simple method for approximating the variance of a complicated estimate." Journal of the American Statistical Association 66:411-414.

EUN SUL LEE is Professor of Biometry and Director of the Office of Health Survey Research and Analysis at School of Public Health, The University of Texas Health Science Center at Houston. He received his undergraduate education at Seoul National University in Korea and his Ph.D. is in Experimental Statistics and Sociology from North Carolina State University. His current research interests involve sample survey design, analysis of health-related survey data, and the application of life table and survival analysis techniques in demography and public health.

RONALD N. FORTHOFER is Professor of Biometry at School of Public Health, The University of Texas Health Science Center at Houston. His Ph.D. is in Biostatistics from the University of North Carolina at Chapel Hill. His research interests involve the application of linear models and categorical data analysis techniques in health research. He is senior author of Public Program Analysis: A New Categorical Data Approach *(with Lehnen, Lifetime Learning Publications, 1981).*

RONALD J. LORIMOR is Associate Professor of Sociology at School of Public Health, The University of Texas Health Science Center at Houston. His Ph.D. is in Sociology from Purdue University. His research interests include methodological issues in survey research and sociodemographic correlates of health status.